JEFFREY DAHMER

By Carla Mooney

AMERICAN CRIME STORIES

An Imprint of Abdo Publishing | abdobooks.com

ABDOBOOKS.COM

Published by Abdo Publishing, a division of ABDO, PO Box 398166, Minneapolis, Minnesota 55439.

Printed in China
102023
012024

Cover Photo: Eugene Garcia/AFP/Getty Images
Interior Photos: Carrie Antlfinger/AP Images, 5, 89; AP Images, 7, 10, 36, 59, 69; Red Line Editorial, 13; Archivio GBB/Alamy, 15, 20; Pool/AP Images, 23; Wikimedia Commons, 25; Curt Borgwardt/Sygma/Getty Images, 27, 84; Steve Kagan/The Chronicle Collection/Getty Images, 33; Dave Schlabowske/AP Images, 35; Sarah L. Voisin/The Washington Post/Getty Images, 41; Photo Researchers/Science History Images/Alamy, 42; KDP/Moment/Getty Images, 45; iStockphoto, 47; Nuccio DiNuzzo/Getty Images News/Getty Images, 49; Shutterstock Images, 50, 77 (folder, jaw, skull, hand, fingerprint, bag, tape), 77 (DNA); Allan Y. Scott/AP Images, 53; Marny Malin/Sygma/Getty Images, 57; Bill Waugh/AP Images, 67; Joe Picciolo/AP Images, 75; Jack Orton/Pool/Milwaukee Journal/AP Images, 81; Ralf-Finn Hestoft/Corbis Historical/Getty Images, 83, 86; Morry Gash/AP Images, 92; Ryan Murphy Productions/Album/Alamy, 96

Editor: Laura Stickney
Series Designer: Melissa Martin

Library of Congress Control Number: 2023939438

PUBLISHER'S CATALOGING-IN-PUBLICATION DATA

Names: Mooney, Carla, author.
Title: Jeffrey Dahmer / by Carla Mooney
Description: Minneapolis, Minnesota: Abdo Publishing, 2024 | Series: American crime stories | Includes online resources and index.
Identifiers: ISBN 9781098292102 (lib. bdg.) | ISBN 9798384910046 (ebook)
Subjects: LCSH: Crime and criminals--Juvenile literature. | Killing (Murder)--Juvenile literature. | United States--Juvenile literature. | Dahmer, Jeffrey--Juvenile literature. | Serial murderers--Juvenile literature. | Wisconsin--Milwaukee--Juvenile literature. | Serial murderers--Juvenile literature.
Classification: DDC 364.97--dc23

CONTENTS

This book discusses accounts of crime, violence, and death that may be disturbing to some readers.

CHAPTER ONE

A GRUESOME DISCOVERY

On July 22, 1991, police officers Rolf Mueller and Robert Rauth worked the 4:00 p.m. to midnight shift in the Third District of Milwaukee, Wisconsin. The Third District included run-down neighborhoods, strip bars, and small grocery stores. Crime in the area was high, with more than half of the city's homicides occurring in the Third District over the previous five years.

Late that night, Mueller and Rauth were sitting in their police patrol car when a short Black man with a handcuff dangling off his wrist approached their car window. The man's appearance may have been unusual in some neighborhoods, but not in the Third District. The nearby Milwaukee County Mental Health Complex kept the local police officers busy with calls about patients involved in all sorts of unusual activities, from directing traffic naked to spray-painting symbols

Jeffrey Dahmer was known to frequent Milwaukee's Third District and the nearby Walker's Point neighborhood.

ESTABLISHED 1985
y Mary
Steny's
TAVERN & GRILL
MILWAUKEE
YOU SHOULD BE HERE!
OPEN
STENY'S PL
ZIM'S

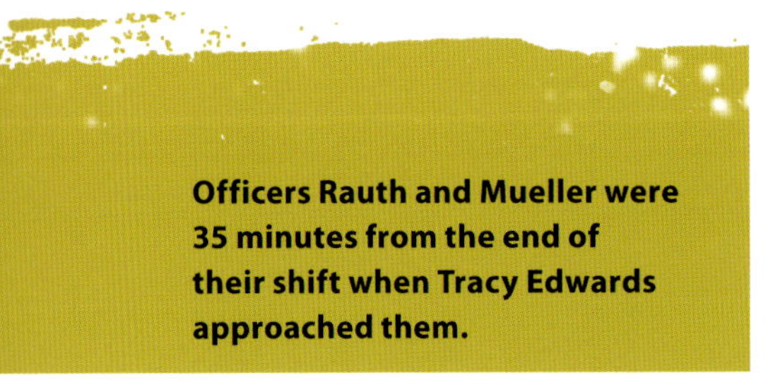
Officers Rauth and Mueller were 35 minutes from the end of their shift when Tracy Edwards approached them.

on houses. "Which one of us did you escape from?" Mueller and Rauth joked to the handcuffed man from their seats inside the patrol car.[1]

An Encounter Gone Bad

Thirty-two-year-old Tracy Edwards stood next to the patrol car and told the two officers about his encounter with a "weird dude."[2] Edwards said he had gone to the man's apartment, where the man put handcuffs on him. At first, the officers told Edwards to get his friend to unlock the handcuffs. But as they listened to Edwards's story, Mueller and Rauth decided it might be a good idea to take a look for themselves. They asked Edwards to take them to the apartment.

Edwards brought the officers to the Oxford Apartments, which was a three-story brick building located at 924 North 25th Street. Most of the building's residents worked and lived quietly, so the police were rarely called there. As soon as they followed Edwards into the apartment building, Mueller and Rauth noticed a heavy, rancid odor. The odor grew stronger as the three men approached the door of apartment 213. At first, the officers thought it was just another one of the odd smells they frequently encountered on the job.

Dahmer lived on the second floor of the Oxford Apartments. The 49-unit building was located near the Marquette University campus.

Apartment 213

When they reached apartment 213, Rauth knocked loudly on the wooden door. "Milwaukee police officers," he shouted.[3] The door opened. The apartment's resident, 31-year-old Jeffrey Dahmer, appeared. Dahmer was a thin man with dark blond hair and a scar over his right eye. He allowed Edwards and the officers to enter his apartment.

Inside, Mueller and Rauth asked Dahmer about the incident with Edwards. Dahmer spoke calmly. The officers hoped that if they could resolve the incident, they could leave without writing a ticket or making an arrest. That way, they could go home on time and avoid extra paperwork. They asked Dahmer to get the key needed to remove the handcuffs.

ROBERT RAUTH

In 1991, 41-year-old Robert Rauth was a 13-year veteran of the Milwaukee Police Department. Rauth was divorced and frequently volunteered for overtime assignments to earn extra money. He was known for his sense of humor. He often kept his fellow police officers laughing with tales of his latest adventures.

Dahmer replied that the key was in the bedroom. But then Edwards spoke up. He accused Dahmer of threatening him with a knife and told the officers that the knife could be found inside the bedroom. Mueller ordered Dahmer to stay where he was. Mueller would go into the bedroom himself to check it out.

A Horrifying Discovery

As soon as Mueller entered the bedroom, he realized that Edwards had been telling the truth. A large knife was underneath the bed. Then Mueller glanced into an open dresser drawer. What he saw inside the drawer stunned him. There were numerous photographs of men in various stages of dismemberment. There were pictures of skulls in kitchen cabinets and refrigerators, and there was even one photo of a human skeleton hanging from a showerhead. Mueller stared at the horrible photographs scattered around the drawer. He struggled to breathe. In a shaky voice, he called out to Rauth. He didn't think this case was going to be resolved quickly anymore.

Up until that point, Dahmer had been calm and polite while talking to the two officers. But when Dahmer realized that he was about to be arrested, his behavior quickly changed. He became violent and began to attack Rauth. The two men wrestled on the floor until Rauth finally managed to subdue Dahmer with handcuffs. Mueller came out of the bedroom, holding several gruesome photographs in his hand. He shakily waved a picture of a severed head at Edwards and told him he was fortunate. "This could have been you," Mueller said to Edwards.[4]

ROLF MUELLER

In 1991, Rolf Mueller was 39 years old and a ten-year veteran of the Milwaukee Police Department. Mueller was born in Germany and moved to the United States as a child. On the night of Dahmer's discovery, Mueller hoped to end his shift on time so he could get home to see his wife and daughter.

Edwards told the two officers about how Dahmer had gotten very upset when Edwards walked toward the refrigerator to get a beer. He weakly joked that maybe Dahmer was hiding a severed head inside the refrigerator. Mueller chuckled at Edwards's outlandish idea and walked over to the refrigerator to show him there was nothing inside of it. Mueller opened the refrigerator door. Then he screamed and quickly slammed the door shut. "Bob, there's a . . . head in the refrigerator!" he yelled to Rauth.[5]

Evidence of Multiple Murders

Mueller's discovery was just the beginning of the gruesome finds in apartment 213. Police found three more human heads in the freezer, neatly packaged in plastic bags tied with plastic twist ties. They also discovered more skulls and dismembered body parts in the refrigerator and other containers. Chemicals such as ethyl alcohol, chloroform, and formaldehyde were stored in the apartment, along with knives, hammers, and saws. Police also found a complete human skeleton, along with a 57-gallon (216 L) vat containing acid, several human torsos, and other body parts.[6] And dozens of photos showed several men in various stages of dismemberment.

Hazardous materials teams helped investigators collect evidence from Dahmer's apartment, including a blue vat that contained acid and human remains.

Police also found videotapes and a mounted video camera in the apartment. The police called in hazardous materials teams to deal with the horrifying discoveries. "You think you've seen it all out here, and then something like this happens," said Mueller in an interview with the *Milwaukee Journal*.[7]

Officers arrested Dahmer and took him to police headquarters. Meanwhile, many of Dahmer's neighbors were stunned by the discoveries in apartment 213. They described Dahmer as a quiet loner who frequently wore the same dirty jeans and T-shirt. They said he often walked in the alley behind the apartment building. Pamela Bass lived across the hall from Dahmer. She noticed his odd behavior, but she didn't think much of it. "I would hear a buzz saw running in the early evening. I thought he was building something," she said.[8]

Many neighbors had complained about the smell of rotten meat or garbage coming from the apartment, and Bass repeatedly asked Dahmer to take care of it. "I would go tell him,

PRESERVED IN GLASS JARS

In Dahmer's apartment, police found body parts from his victims preserved in glass jars and formaldehyde. This is a colorless, flammable, strong-smelling chemical. Solutions of formaldehyde mixed with water are one type of preservative fluid. Scientists use these solutions to preserve specimens, such as reptiles, amphibians, and fish, for long-term storage.

'Jeff, something's stinking again.' He would say it was the rotten meat in his freezer. He even bought a bunch of Pine Sol once, like he was really going to get rid of it this time. But it didn't help," she said.[9]

A Notorious Serial Killer

Over the next two weeks, detectives questioned Dahmer for 60 hours. He confessed to killing and dismembering 17 men and boys between 1978 and 1991. On July 25, 1991, police officially charged Dahmer with four counts of first-degree murder.[10]

Investigators continued working to identify more of Dahmer's victims and build a case against him. As they gathered more evidence, they charged him with additional murders. Eventually, Dahmer was charged with a total of 15 counts of first-degree murder in Wisconsin and one count in Ohio.[11] Since his arrest, Jeffrey Lionel Dahmer has become one of the most notorious serial killers in history.

DAHMER'S VICTIMS

In total, Dahmer confessed to murdering 17 people.

NAME	AGE	DATE KILLED
Steven Hicks	18	June 18, 1978
Steven Tuomi	24	November 20, 1987
Jamie Doxtator	14	January 16, 1988
Richard Guerrero	25	March 24, 1988
Anthony Sears	26	March 25, 1989
Raymond Smith (Ricky Lee Beeks)	33	May 20, 1990
Edward W. Smith	28	June 1990
Ernest Miller	22	September 1990
David C. Thomas	23	September 24, 1990
Curtis Straughter	18	February 18, 1991
Errol Lindsey	19	April 7, 1991
Anthony "Tony" Hughes	31	May 24, 1991
Konerak Sinthasomphone	14	May 27, 1991
Matt Turner	20	June 30, 1991
Jeremiah Weinberger	23	July 5, 1991
Oliver Lacy	23	July 15, 1991
Joseph Bradehoft	25	July 19, 1991

CHAPTER TWO

TROUBLES AS A CHILD

Jeffrey Dahmer was born in Milwaukee, Wisconsin, on May 21, 1960. He was the first child of chemist Lionel Dahmer and his wife Joyce, a homemaker. In Jeffrey's earliest years, there were few clues that he would become a killer. However, as Jeffrey grew older, people around him began noticing his odd characteristics and unusual activities.

Feelings of Neglect

When Jeffrey was six years old, his family moved from Wisconsin to Barberton, Ohio. In December 1966, the Dahmers welcomed a second son, David. Adding a new baby to the family may have caused Jeffrey to feel ignored. At the time, Jeffrey was in first grade at Hazel Harvey Elementary School. Jeffrey became more withdrawn after his brother

A 1964 photo shows Jeffrey Dahmer at age four. Some people wonder if the neglect Jeffrey experienced from a young age contributed to his later behavior.

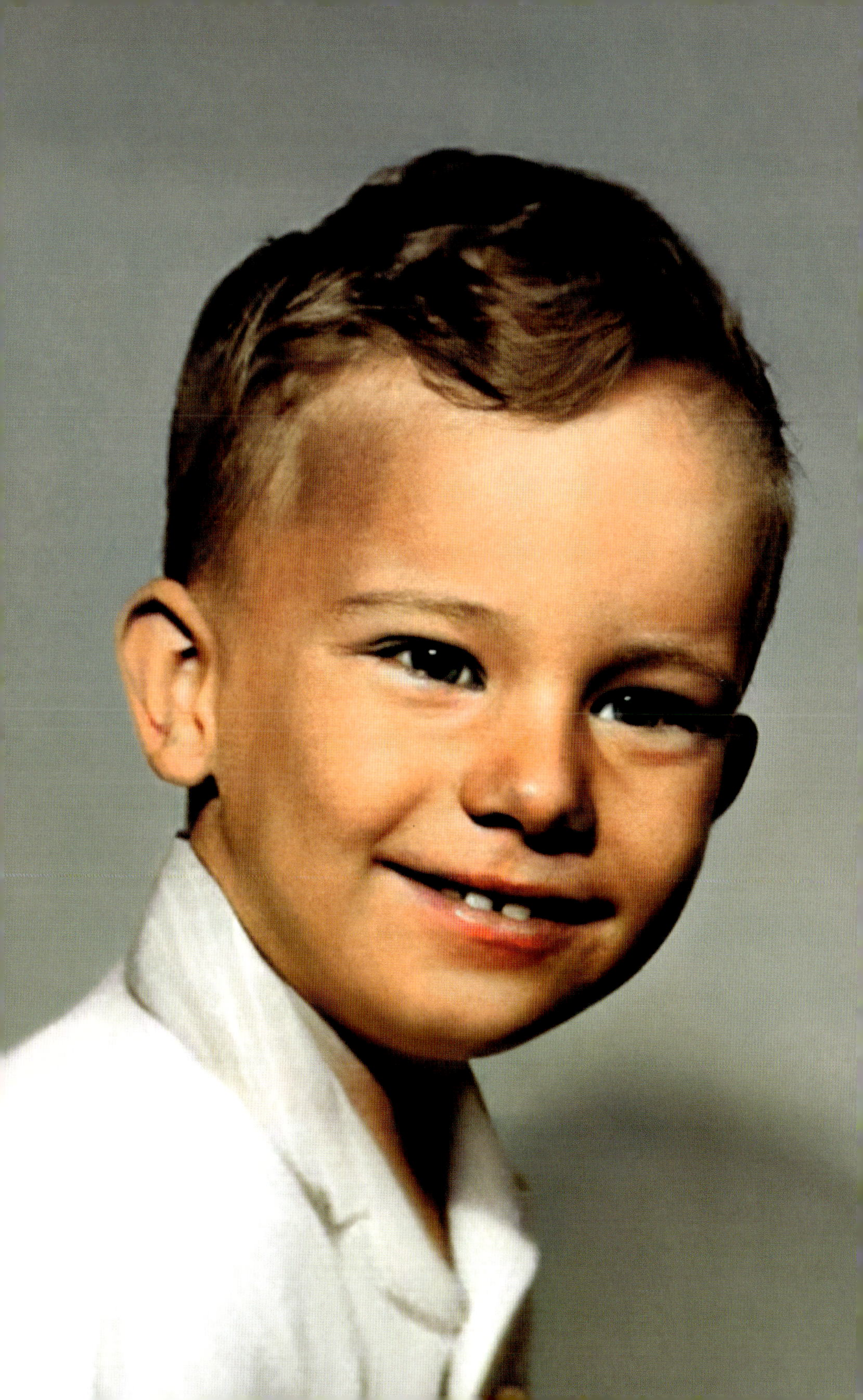

was born. He may have felt like he was not getting enough attention from his parents at home. His teacher noticed the changes in Jeffrey's demeanor at school and wrote on his report card that the first grader appeared to feel neglected.

In 1968, when Jeffrey was eight years old, the Dahmers moved to Bath, Ohio. They moved into a large ranch-style house on 1.7 wooded acres (0.7 ha).[1] Jeffrey enrolled in the local school, Bath Elementary School. But life at the Dahmer family home during this time was not ideal. Joyce had multiple mental health issues, including postpartum depression, after David's birth. Lionel struggled to work through the problems with his wife, often spending time at work or otherwise away from home. This meant that Joyce had to care for her two boys alone for long periods of time. Sometimes things got so bad that Lionel would wake up in the middle of the night to discover Joyce lying outside in a field in her nightgown. But Lionel never talked about Joyce's problems with Jeffrey or David.

HERNIA SURGERY

At age four, Jeffrey had surgery for a double hernia on his groin. The experience was likely terrifying, and it is unknown if anyone took the time to explain to young Jeffrey what was happening to him. Later, Jeffrey's father said he was convinced that the operation caused his son to distrust the world around him, eventually leading him to murder.

ALLEGED ASSAULT

In 1991, Lionel Dahmer told his son's probation agents that Jeffrey had been sexually assaulted by a neighborhood boy when he was eight years old. The alleged assault was never reported to police. Lionel believed the assault may have contributed to Jeffrey's issues with sexuality as a teen and adult. However, Dahmer consistently denied that the assault ever happened.

Experimenting with Animals

Jeffrey became interested in chemistry. When he was in elementary school, Lionel gave him a chemistry set. Jeffrey experimented with chemicals and learned how they affected insects and small animals. At first, he collected insects and used chemicals to preserve them in jars. Later, he began collecting animals that had been hit by cars.

Dahmer once showed a classmate a stuffed taxidermy squirrel and told the student that he always wanted to do the same thing to a human.

Jeffrey cut off the heads of these animals and mounted them on sticks in the woods behind his home. He collected dried-out animal skins and animal bones. He even created an animal burial ground with graves and small crosses in his backyard. Eric Tyson lived across the street from the Dahmers. He remembered the chipmunk and squirrel skeletons that Jeffrey kept in his shed. "A number

SIGNS OF A SERIAL KILLER

Behavioral experts note that serial killers like Dahmer often exhibit warning signs from a young age. Potential warning signs include extreme antisocial behavior, an interest in watching people undress without their knowledge, a fascination with setting fires, and killing or harming animals without remorse. While these signs do not predict who will become a serial killer, they can identify people with an elevated chance of engaging in serial violence. However, mental illness is not itself an indicator of violent behavior.

of neighbors have recalled seeing animals, like frogs and cats, impaled or staked to trees," he said.[2]

According to experts, this behavior with animals may have been an early clue to Jeffrey's future killings. "Murderers like this very often start out by killing and torturing animals as kids," said Robert K. Ressler.[3] Ressler developed profiles of serial killers as an agent with the Federal Bureau of Investigation (FBI).

Jeffrey was also intrigued by the insides of animals. He carefully removed the skins from animal specimens and dissolved them in chemicals to study the animals' insides. Neighborhood children remember that while fishing, Jeffrey chopped his fish into little pieces to examine its insides. The children also reported that Jeffrey liked to put his head against their chests to hear their heartbeats. "Everybody has a kid in their class that's a little different, a little bit strange. You just kind of brush it off because he's going to outgrow it, or he's just going through a stage," said Steve Lehr, one of Jeffrey's childhood playmates and neighbors.[4]

High School Years

In 1974, Jeffrey started classes at Revere High School. During his high school years, he earned average grades. Jeffrey also played clarinet in the high school band, participated in tennis, and worked on the school newspaper.

Classmates remember Jeffrey as a heavy drinker and an odd loner. Martha Schmidt recalls an interaction with Jeffrey during their sophomore year of high school. Jeffrey sat next to her holding a Styrofoam cup filled with scotch. When she asked him about it, he told her it was his "medicine."[5]

According to his former classmates, Dahmer could also be a class clown with an unusual sense of humor. He would reportedly yell odd things in public places. Sometimes he pretended to faint. In 1978, Dahmer snuck into the National Honor Society yearbook photo, even though he was not a member of the honor society. "It was a very Jeff thing to do," explained Schmidt. "It was part of his trying to be unconventional and to mock everything around him. I think he very consciously chose the honor society because I think in some ways he was laughing at himself and us."[6]

When kids at Dahmer's high school acted silly or stupid, they called it "doing a Dahmer."[7]

In 1978, Dahmer was a senior at Revere High School. Classmates recall Dahmer drinking alcohol at school and pulling pranks.

Trouble at Home

Meanwhile, Lionel and Joyce Dahmer's marriage was in trouble. The couple fought constantly, and Lionel moved into a different part of the house to escape his wife. Later, he moved out of the home and into a motel. Eventually, the couple filed for divorce.

During Jeffrey's senior year of high school, his parents were in the middle of their bitter divorce. One of the main issues was a battle for custody of Jeffrey's younger brother, David.

Because Jeffrey was already 18 years old, he was not part of the custody battle. Eventually, the court awarded custody of David to Joyce. The Dahmers' divorce was finalized on July 24, 1978.

First Murder Occurs

While Lionel and Joyce Dahmer were focused on their divorce, their son's attention was elsewhere. Dahmer was often left alone at the family home. His mother had taken his little brother and moved back to Wisconsin, leaving Dahmer with his father. Lionel had already started dating another woman and spent many hours at his job. That summer, Dahmer spent a lot of time by himself and became increasingly lonely. He hated being alone in the house at night and began feeling strongly about being left behind. He also began to fantasize about killing people. Dahmer later explained to police that these fantasies helped him deal with his feelings of emptiness and frustration.

Dahmer graduated from high school in June 1978. A few days later, on June 18, 18-year-old Steven Hicks went to a rock concert in Chippewa Lake Park, Ohio. After the concert, Hicks decided to hitchhike home. Dahmer saw Hicks, offered him a ride, and invited him back to his home for some beers. The two young men got drunk and started making out.

But things turned violent when Hicks attempted to leave Dahmer's house. Dahmer begged him to stay, but Hicks insisted on leaving. Dahmer said the two men got into a physical fight and traded punches. Dahmer reached for a nearby dumbbell and struck Hicks on the back of the head with the heavy weight. As Hicks lay motionless on the floor, Dahmer tried to wake him. But Hicks was dead. Later, Dahmer explained that he killed Hicks because he did not want Hicks to leave him.

Dahmer realized he needed to dispose of Hicks's body. He dragged the body into a crawl space under his house. There, he used a kitchen knife to cut the body into pieces. Then he placed the body parts in plastic bags. At first, Dahmer kept the bags in his car. But then he decided it would be better to bury them in the woods behind his house. Later, Dahmer dug up the bags. He used a sledgehammer to break the bones into pieces and then scattered them in the woods. Dahmer also burned Hicks's wallet, cut up Hicks's necklace, and threw the knife he had used to dismember the body into a nearby river.

On June 24, 1978, Hicks's mother, Martha Hicks, reported her son missing. Police retraced Hicks's movements from the rock concert and interviewed many of his friends and relatives. A reward was offered for information leading to his return, but for years, no one knew what had happened to Steven Hicks.

A Confession

Once Dahmer was arrested in 1991, he confessed the details of his first murder to Milwaukee police. The Milwaukee police contacted Ohio police to see if there was an open case for a missing hitchhiker from 1978. They said yes. The missing person case of Steven Hicks had remained unsolved for more than a decade.

Police traveled to Milwaukee to question Dahmer about Hicks. When they showed him a picture of Hicks, Dahmer identified the hitchhiker. Dahmer also drew a map for investigators that led them to Hicks's remains on the old Dahmer property in Bath, Ohio. Dahmer was officially charged with the murder of Hicks on September 17, 1991.

Investigators found more than 50 pieces of bone, including skull pieces, while searching the Dahmer property for Hicks's remains.

CHAPTER THREE

A CONFUSED YOUNG ADULT

In the fall of 1978, Dahmer enrolled at Ohio State University. It seemed like a normal next step for the high school graduate. Yet no one at home or at school knew about the deadly secret Dahmer had buried in his family's backyard.

College Life

Dahmer was one of 43,000 students enrolled at Ohio State University that fall, according to records from the university registrar's office.[1] He moved into a room in Morrill Tower with other male students on his floor. He did not declare a major, entering the university as an undecided student. Dahmer signed up for several classes during his first semester, including Introduction to Anthropology, Greco-Roman History, and Riflery.

While at Ohio State University, Dahmer lived in room 541 of Morrill Tower. He reportedly stole things from his roommates and sold them at a local pawn shop.

Dahmer's drinking, which had started in high school, quickly worsened in college. In 1978, the legal drinking age in Ohio was 18 for low-alcohol beers. However, getting higher alcohol-content beers or mixed drinks at bars was not difficult. Dahmer often skipped class and spent his time drinking at local bars. "He would wake up in the morning, not go to class. He would instead go down to the dining hall. At the time, he would eat by himself, then walk to south campus at the bars down there," said Jessica Langer, who served as editor of the *Lantern*, Ohio State's student newspaper, more than 40 years after Dahmer attended the school.[2] In 2022, Langer researched Dahmer's time at the university. When Dahmer went to class, he was often drunk and sometimes even brought a liquor bottle with him. He rarely turned in class assignments.

High school classmate John "Derf" Backderf believed that Dahmer turned to alcohol as a way to deal with mental issues and emotions he struggled to understand. "Dahmer was a complete mess by this point," said Backderf. "The memory of what he had done to Stephen Hicks both tortured him and [excited] him. His ghastly sexual obsessions were taking him over, body and soul, and driving him insane."[3]

In 2012, Dahmer's high school classmate John Backderf wrote an acclaimed graphic novel called *My Friend Dahmer*. It is about the serial killer's early years.

Lionel and Shari Dahmer would go on to talk about Jeffrey on talk shows and in interviews.

Dahmer's father gave him a weekly allowance, but Dahmer spent it all at the local bars. When he ran out of money, he donated plasma at local blood banks to earn money to pay for alcohol. Dahmer was also suspected of several campus thefts and was questioned by police, but no charges were filed.

Dahmer spent only a few months at Ohio State. He did not do well in his classes. According to his father, Dahmer earned a grade point average of 0.45. By December 1978, Dahmer had dropped out of the university.

A New Stepmother

While Dahmer struggled at Ohio State, more change occurred in his family life. In December 1978, Lionel married Shari Jordan.

According to Shari, she noticed Dahmer's vulnerability and wanted to "mother" him.[4] But neighbors have a slightly different recollection of the family, with some reporting that Shari wanted little to do with her two new stepsons.

Shari and Lionel recognized that Dahmer had a drinking problem. When Shari moved into Lionel's house, her liquor bottles mysteriously disappeared, and she suspected Dahmer was stealing them. Once, Dahmer got so drunk that he forgot where he had left his father's car, and Lionel and Shari had to find it. Since college had not helped Dahmer get his life together, Lionel and Shari suggested that he try another path: the military.

Time in the Military

With the encouragement of his father and stepmother, Dahmer enlisted in the US Army. He never wanted to be a soldier, but he thought joining the army would make his father happy. He also hoped the change of scenery would help him forget Hicks.

On January 12, 1979, Dahmer reported for duty at Fort McClellan in Anniston, Alabama. At first, Dahmer trained to be a military police officer. Later, he transferred to Fort Sam Houston in San Antonio, Texas. There, Dahmer took a six-week class for medical specialists, a job similar to a nurse's aide. After completing training, Private First Class Dahmer was sent to Baumholder, West Germany, in July 1979. He was assigned to the army's Second Battalion, Sixty-eighth Armored Regiment, Eighth Infantry Division, as a combat medic.

Dahmer was rated as an "average or slightly above average" soldier during his first year in the army.[5] But his drinking problems continued. His bunkmates at Baumholder said he turned a suitcase into a minibar stocked with a martini shaker, stirrer, and more. On the weekends, Dahmer usually made drinks for himself and listened to heavy metal music on his headphones until he passed out drunk. At one point, Dahmer's bunkmates took a photo of him passed out on his bed after one of his drinking sessions. Sometimes, he would disappear for an entire weekend.

Dahmer's fellow soldiers at Baumholder said he rarely spoke about his family. He mostly kept to himself, with occasional outbursts when he was drunk. Some of his outbursts involved racial slurs toward Black soldiers. One bunkmate, Billy Capshaw, said Dahmer had a violent streak when he was drunk. "When he'd drink, he'd get real violent with me. You could tell in his face that he

ACCUSATIONS

After Dahmer's arrest in 1991, two men who served with him in the military came forward and accused him of assaulting them while in Germany. Preston Davis accused Dahmer of drugging and assaulting him on a field exercise in Belgium. Dahmer's roommate Billy Capshaw accused Dahmer of beating, torturing, and assaulting him multiple times during his time in Germany.

wasn't joking. It was for real. That's why it bothered me. It was a whole different side. His face was blank. It was kind of like he was cross-eyed-like. An expression like he just wasn't there. I've never seen it on anyone else's face," said Capshaw.[6]

Another fellow soldier remembered that Dahmer used to talk about killing someone in Ohio when he got drunk. But the other soldiers did not believe him. "He would get drunk in the barracks and say, 'I killed the guy in Ohio,' and we'd say, 'You didn't kill nobody!'" said Preston Davis, who was stationed with Dahmer in Baumholder. "He became a monster once he started drinking. Alcohol is what turned him into a monster," Davis explained.[7]

Army Discharge

Eventually, Dahmer's drinking problem affected his military performance so much that his commanding officers could no longer ignore it. Dahmer also struggled with his work as a medical specialist because he got squeamish when doing more than taking a patient's blood pressure. He told his superiors that he disliked pricking patients to draw blood. On March 24, 1981, Dahmer was discharged under an army regulation involving alcohol and drug abuse. His discharge occurred nine months before the end of his enlistment period. As he packed to return home to the United States, Dahmer joked with his fellow soldiers. He told them, "Someday, you'll hear about me again."[8]

When Dahmer left Germany, his squad leader, David G. Goss, drove him to the airport. Goss remembered thinking that something was bothering Dahmer during his time in Germany. "I knew he had a troubled past, and I knew he had something that was gnawing at him. He'd say there was something he could not talk about," said Goss.[9] At the time, none of Dahmer's superiors in the army thought his drinking would significantly impact his ability to live as a civilian.

UNSOLVED MURDERS IN GERMANY

After Dahmer's arrest in 1991, German police looked at five unsolved murders that occurred when he was in Germany. No evidence linking him to the murders was ever found, and Dahmer told detectives he had never killed anyone in Germany.

Back in the States

After his army discharge, Dahmer moved to Miami, Florida, and got a job working at a sandwich shop. He later told police that his time in Florida was uneventful, with no murders taking place there. Less than a year after arriving in Florida, Dahmer moved back to Ohio to live with his father and stepmother.

But Dahmer's behavior started causing problems again. On October 7, 1981, Dahmer got drunk at Maxwell's Lounge, a motel bar at the Ramada Inn in Bath, Ohio. When he refused to

MISSING: ADAM WALSH

In July 1981, six-year-old Adam Walsh was kidnapped from a department store in Hollywood, Florida. On August 10, Adam's head was found about 120 miles (193 km) away. But the rest of his body was never found. During this time, Dahmer was living in Miami Beach, less than 20 miles (32 km) from Hollywood.[10] Although Dahmer denied being involved in Walsh's disappearance and murder, some people believe Dahmer may have killed the young boy.

leave the bar, Bath police arrested him. They charged him with disorderly conduct, having an open container of alcohol, and resisting arrest.

Lionel grew increasingly worried about his son's excessive drinking. He knew that Dahmer stayed out late at the bars, frequently demanding more drinks as he got drunk. Sometimes Dahmer got into fights that led to stitches and broken ribs. Lionel strongly believed that his son needed a change of environment to help him get his life on track.

After some thought, Lionel came up with what he believed to be the perfect solution. He sent Dahmer to West Allis, Wisconsin, to live with Dahmer's grandmother. Dahmer could help his elderly grandmother with chores around the house. And Wisconsin would give him the opportunity for a fresh start.

Lionel Dahmer described his son as "extremely shy" and said that he was unaware of his son's interest in dead animals.

CHAPTER FOUR

NEW START IN WISCONSIN

In early 1982, Dahmer moved in with his grandmother, Catherine Dahmer, in West Allis, Wisconsin. Catherine Dahmer lived in a two-story house in a neighborhood of mainly working-class people. Her home had a separate entrance that led to the basement. This would give Dahmer the privacy he would need to carry out some of his early murders.

Catherine Dahmer was a religious woman. She regularly attended a Lutheran church and was kind and loving to her grandson. She encouraged Dahmer to attend church services and weekday prayer meetings with her. At first, Dahmer hoped that by surrounding himself with religion, he could push away the memory of Steven Hicks and keep his drinking under control. He also hoped church activities could help him overcome his sexual fantasies. At this point, Dahmer knew he was gay, but he did not tell his grandmother. He knew

Catherine Dahmer's house was located in a suburban area. Jeffrey was reportedly closer to his grandmother than to anyone else in his family.

she would not understand, and it would not be accepted at her church.

At first, Dahmer tried to use his time at his grandmother's house to reset his life. He got a job at the Milwaukee Blood Plasma Center. Here, he used his medical specialist skills to draw blood from donors, despite having previously told the army that he disliked pricking people. He hoped going to work and

Dahmer was arrested in 1982 for exposing himself to a group of 25 people, including women and children.

attending church would help him suppress his attraction to men.

In August 1982, Dahmer was arrested at the Wisconsin State Fair for drunk and disorderly conduct. Police also reported that he lowered his pants in front of several people. Dahmer was fined $50 for these actions.[1]

After his arrest at the state fair, Dahmer managed to stay out of trouble for a few years. He helped his grandmother with chores and yard work. In January 1985, Dahmer landed a new job at the Ambrosia Chocolate Company, where he worked as a mixer. But Dahmer later admitted to police that when he moved to Wisconsin, his teenage fantasies about killing people returned.

AMBROSIA CHOCOLATE COMPANY

Dahmer's job at the Ambrosia Chocolate Company paid $8.25 per hour to start. Dahmer frequently worked the overnight shift, from 11:00 p.m. to 7:30 a.m.[2] On this shift, there were fewer supervisors. And he did not have to be in contact with the public, which pleased him. Dahmer would remain employed with the company for six years, one of the few stable parts of his life. The company moved locations about a year after Dahmer's arrest. The original building was torn down.

The Club Scene

In an interview with detectives after his 1991 arrest, Dahmer told a story about meeting a young man at the library in Wauwatosa, Wisconsin. He said the man walked by and gave him a note suggesting Dahmer meet with him to make out. Dahmer felt that moment was a turning point in his life and that he was wasting his time trying to live according to his grandmother's religious rules. Instead, Dahmer says he realized he was not fooling anyone. At that point, he decided to seek dates with men.

Dahmer began to frequent Milwaukee's gay bars and clubs. Most of the time, he sat at the bar and drank. He did not have a car, so he often took a cab or bus home. Usually, his grandmother was asleep when he got home, so she did not give him too much trouble about being drunk. At the gay bars, Dahmer found it easy to meet other gay men, some of whom he brought back to his grandmother's basement. On other occasions, he and a date would spend the night at a hotel downtown.

In 1986, Dahmer once again committed sexual misconduct. He was arrested for lewd behavior after exposing himself to two 12-year-old boys in Milwaukee. Dahmer confessed to police officers that it was not the first time he had done this. He had exposed himself in public about five times in the past few months.[3] Dahmer told police that he did not know why he started doing this. He said he recognized that he had a problem and needed to get help. The police reduced the charges to disorderly conduct, and Dahmer was sentenced to one year of probation and therapy.

Dahmer also began to visit the Club Baths in Milwaukee, a bathhouse where gay men went to meet others. During the summer of 1987, Dahmer was accused of drugging men at the bathhouse. Police came to the bathhouse and interviewed employees and customers, including Dahmer. However, because no one wanted to file charges, nothing happened.

Another Murder

In November 1987, nine years after his first murder, Dahmer killed his second victim. According to Dahmer's later confession, he met Steven Tuomi, a young white man who was about 25 years old, at Club 219. This was one of Milwaukee's popular gay bars. The pair rented a room at the Ambassador Hotel, where they got drunk and passed out.

Dahmer told investigators that when he woke up, Tuomi was dead, although Dahmer had no memory of killing him. Dahmer's hands and arms were bruised and sore, while Tuomi had bruises and blood on his face and chest. Dahmer assumed

CLUB 219

Club 219 opened in Milwaukee around 1981. For many years, the club was a hot spot for dancing, with bright lights, loud music, and high-energy dance parties. It also hosted regular drag show performances, male strippers, and dancers. By the mid-1990s, the club's popularity began to wane, especially once people learned of its connection to Dahmer. It closed in October 2005.

that he must have beaten Tuomi to death, even though he didn't remember doing it. Dahmer cleaned himself up and devised a plan to get rid of Tuomi's body.

Dahmer called a cab and went to a nearby mall to buy a suitcase. "I bought the biggest suitcase I could find. It was the kind that had the size zipper feature, making it easy to fill with large items," he said. Back at the hotel, Dahmer stuffed Tuomi's body into the suitcase. "I know it sounds strange, but the guy folded right into the thing, just like it was designed for him. The cab driver helped me carry everything out to the car and placed the suitcase into the trunk," said Dahmer.[4] The cab drove Dahmer and the suitcase back to his grandmother's house.

At his grandmother's house, Dahmer carried the suitcase down into the basement. It was Thanksgiving Day, and his family had already arrived. So Dahmer left the body in the suitcase and went upstairs to join his family for the holiday dinner. No one suspected anything was wrong.

The next day, after his family had left and his grandmother had gone out with friends, Dahmer decided it was time to get rid of Tuomi's body. He took the body out of the suitcase and placed it over a drain on the basement floor. Using a kitchen knife, Dahmer cut the body into pieces. Then he put the pieces in plastic bags and threw them out in garbage bags. He cleaned the floor and poured bleach down the drain to get rid of any evidence of his crime.

Dahmer murdered Tuomi in room 507 of the Ambassador Hotel.

A New Plan

Now Dahmer had killed two men. As far as he could tell, he had gotten away with it. His emotions swung from feeling terrified of being caught to feeling exhilarated at getting away with murder. Just thinking about the murders gave him pleasure. Dahmer had his secret, and the knowledge made him feel powerful. He decided to kill again, but he would plan it in advance this time.

Dahmer had heard about a drug called Halcion that could be used to help people sleep. He went to a doctor and persuaded the doctor to write him a prescription for the sleeping medication. Halcion worked quickly and put him to sleep right away. Dahmer wondered how the drug might work on his late-night dates. He planned to use the drug on his next victim.

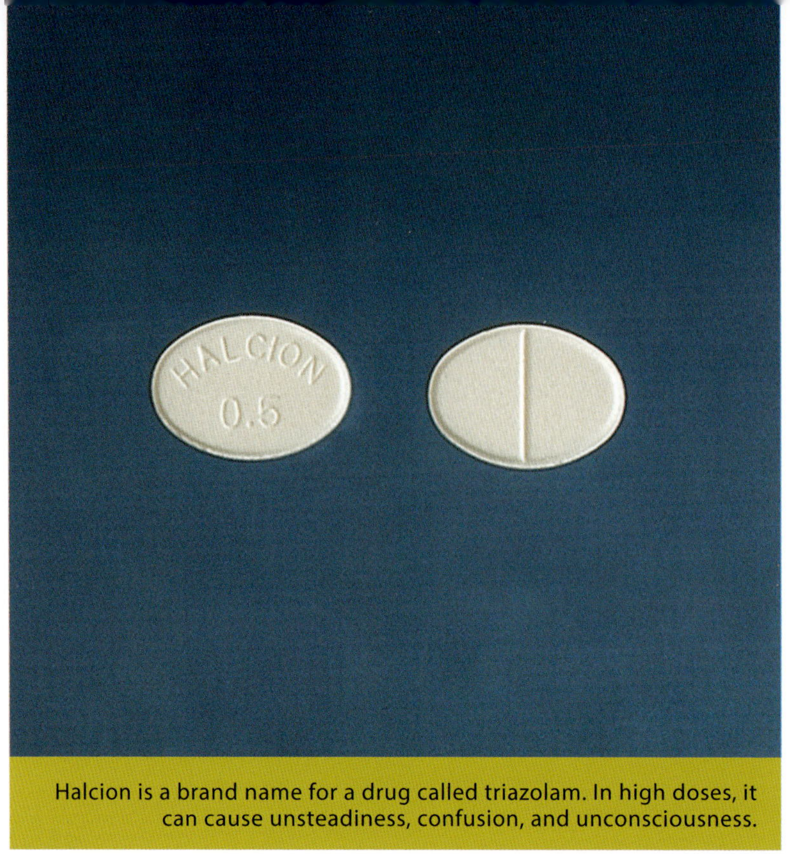

Halcion is a brand name for a drug called triazolam. In high doses, it can cause unsteadiness, confusion, and unconsciousness.

About two months after Tuomi's murder, Dahmer met 14-year-old James Doxtator at a bus stop outside Club 219. Dahmer invited Doxtator over to his grandmother's house to drink and watch videos. Doxtator agreed, and he and Dahmer went to Catherine Dahmer's house. In the basement, Dahmer handed Doxtator a drink with crushed Halcion tablets in it. Within 15 minutes, Doxtator passed out cold. Dahmer raped the unconscious youth. To prevent Doxtator from telling anyone about being drugged, Dahmer decided to kill him. He strangled the unconscious Doxtator with his bare hands.

Dahmer hid Doxtator's body in the basement fruit cellar. The next day, while his grandmother was at church, Dahmer used a knife to cut Doxtator's body into pieces near a drain in the basement floor. He used a sledgehammer to break the bones. He put the bones and body parts into plastic bags and tossed them into the trash. "I almost couldn't believe what I did, yet just thinking about it gave me great pleasure," Dahmer said in a 1991 police interview.[5]

A Fourth Victim

Dahmer monitored the local newspaper and television news reports regarding the missing men. However, there was nothing. No one even knew they were missing. It was exciting to him, so Dahmer decided to kill again.

In March 1988, Dahmer met his fourth victim, a 25-year-old man named Richard Guerrero. Guerrero was a young man of Mexican heritage. Dahmer said he met Guerrero at the Phoenix Bar in Milwaukee's gay bar district. Dahmer followed a familiar pattern and invited Guerrero back to his house to take photographs and watch videos. In the basement, Dahmer drugged Guerrero by giving

PROBATION ENDS

On March 10, 1988, Dahmer reported in for the last time to his probation officer. On March 20, 1988, Wisconsin's Division of Corrections declared that Dahmer had satisfied all conditions of his one-year probation for his disorderly conduct charge. He was discharged and no longer had to report to anyone. Four days later, he killed his fourth victim.

him a drink with sleeping pills in it. After the young man fell asleep, Dahmer strangled him to death.

The next day, Dahmer dismembered Guerrero's body and disposed of the pieces in garbage bags as he had done previously. He later admitted to detectives that he experienced mixed feelings about his activities. "I loved having these guys with me . . . but after killing them, I felt empty, and the task of disposing [of] their bodies was no easy job. When it was done, I felt empty and alone," he said.[6] For a little while, Dahmer tried to meet men and have relationships with them. But he always felt alone when the men left him.

Growing Frustration

Although Catherine Dahmer was unaware of the gruesome activities happening in her basement, she grew increasingly frustrated with her grandson. She thought he spent too much time drinking, going to bars, and hanging out with strange men at all hours of the night. Even worse, she was disturbed by the peculiar smells coming from the basement. When Catherine complained about the foul odors, Dahmer dismissed her concerns, claiming they came from his taxidermy hobby.

But Catherine was still uncomfortable. She asked her son Lionel to talk to Dahmer about finding another place to live. Catherine also wanted Lionel to ask Dahmer about an unusual black substance leaking from one of the outside garbage cans.

Dahmer often disposed of his victims' remains in garbage bags. Once, he was even pulled over by police while a victim' remains were in trash bags in the back seat of his car. The police did not search the bags and let Dahmer drive away.

Dahmer explained to his father that he had been using chemicals to remove the skin from dead animals, just as he had done with his chemistry set as a child. Lionel quickly accepted his son's explanation.

In September 1988, Dahmer moved out of Catherine's house into a dingy apartment building in Milwaukee. The new living arrangement would not last long. Dahmer would live there for only a month before committing further crimes.

CHAPTER FIVE

ALMOST CAUGHT

In late September 1988, Dahmer moved into an apartment in a run-down brick building on North 24th Street in Milwaukee. A day later, he found a new victim to target: a 13-year-old Laotian boy named Somsack Sinthasomphone, who went to school a block away from Dahmer's apartment building. Dahmer lured the boy using a method that had worked well for him: offering to pay him to model in photos.

Dahmer asked Somsack if he would help test a camera and offered him $50 to pose for photos. The boy agreed and followed Dahmer to his apartment. Once inside, Dahmer persuaded the boy to remove some of his clothing. Dahmer took a few pictures and told the teen to look "sexier" for the photos.[1] He also kissed the boy's stomach and touched his genitals.

Meanwhile, Dahmer offered the boy coffee with Irish cream liqueur. He had crushed up sleeping pills and mixed them

Dahmer often asked his victims to model in photos. He also took pictures of his victims' dead bodies. Police would later find approximately 80 Polaroid photos in Dahmer's apartment.

2-4 FT
.6-1.2M
4FT-∞
1.2M-∞
600 Film

into the coffee. When Somsack left and went home, his family noticed something was wrong. He could not walk without bumping into furniture and seemed confused and incoherent. Then the boy passed out.

His family tried to wake him but failed. They rushed Somsack to the hospital. Tests revealed that the boy had been drugged. The hospital doctors called the police to alert them. When Somsack regained consciousness, he told police where he had gone with Dahmer.

Questioned by Police

Police tracked Dahmer down at the chocolate factory and brought him to the police station for questioning. Meanwhile, they also searched Dahmer's apartment. They collected evidence, including a coffee cup with traces of the drug and liquor, a prescription for the sedative, and a camera.

When questioned by detectives, Dahmer tried to explain that he did not know Somsack's age and thought he was older. He also denied kissing or touching the boy inappropriately. When asked about the drugs in the boy's system, Dahmer explained that it was an accident. He told the police he used the same coffee cup to take his prescription medicine. Because he was the only person living in the apartment, Dahmer said he did not always wash the cup and suggested that there must have been some residue from his medication in the

Before Dahmer's 1991 arrest, Milwaukee police officers questioned Dahmer four times and even entered his apartment. But they never uncovered the truth about his crimes.

cup, which would explain how the drugs got into Somsack's system. Dahmer insisted that the boy was fine when he left the apartment.

The police did not believe Dahmer's explanations. They arrested Dahmer and charged him with the sexual exploitation of a child and second-degree sexual assault. The court set bail at $10,000.[2] Lionel Dahmer paid his son's bail to get him out of jail and hired a defense attorney to represent him. In January 1989, Dahmer pleaded guilty in court, and his sentencing was scheduled for May 23, 1989. As he waited for sentencing, Dahmer remained out on bail. He returned to live at his grandmother's house.

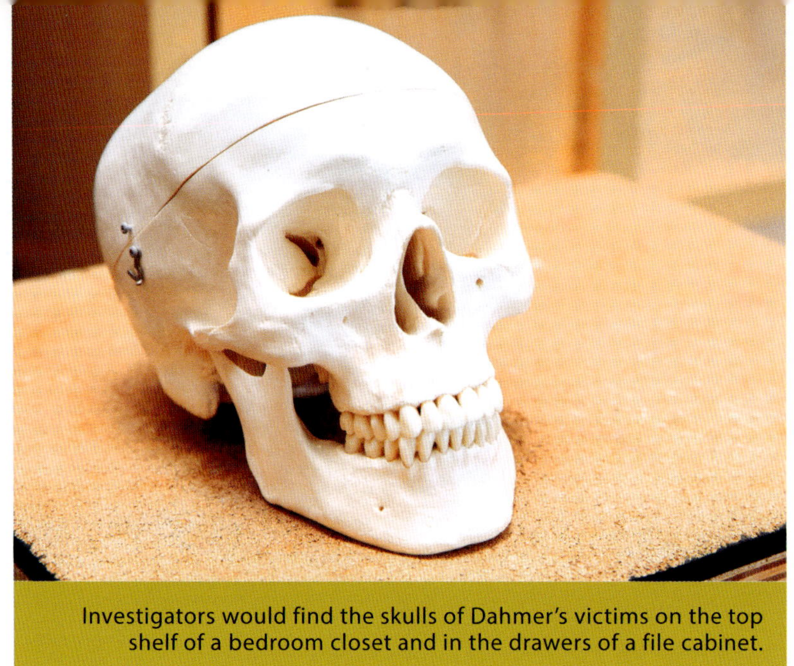

Investigators would find the skulls of Dahmer's victims on the top shelf of a bedroom closet and in the drawers of a file cabinet.

Murder Again

While on bail, Dahmer returned to Milwaukee's gay bars. In March 1989, he met a young Black man named Anthony Sears at La Cage Aux Folles, a popular gay bar in the area. Sears worked as a restaurant manager, but he dreamed of becoming a model and loved to have his picture taken. A friend said he last saw Sears on March 25. Sears was seen with Dahmer near Catherine Dahmer's house.

Later, Dahmer said that he had told Sears he lived in Chicago and had come to Milwaukee to visit his grandmother. He offered to pay Sears to take pictures and invited him back to Catherine's home. In the basement, the men had sex. Then Dahmer drugged Sears with sleeping pills. As he had done several times before, Dahmer strangled the sleeping man and dismembered his body.

But this time, Dahmer strayed from his usual pattern. He kept Sears's head. Dahmer boiled the head in hot water and soap to remove the skin and flesh. Then he painted the skull gray so it would look like a model used by medical students. It was the first time Dahmer saved a body part from one of his victims, but it would not be the last. Dahmer kept the skull for two years until police recovered it in 1991. In interviews with detectives in 1991, Dahmer explained why he kept the skulls of some of his victims, saying, "I wanted to keep those guys with me."[3]

Meanwhile, in the aftermath of his crimes against Somsack, Dahmer met with a psychologist assigned to him by the Department of Probation and Parole. Before his sentencing, Dahmer's bail monitor wrote a letter to the sentencing judge. In the letter, the bail monitor noted that Dahmer had become more relaxed, verbal, and friendly since meeting with the psychologist. He seemed more willing to participate in community events instead of isolating himself at home.

Sentencing Hearing

Judge William Gardner presided over Dahmer's sentencing on May 23, 1989. Assistant District Attorney Gale Shelton was an 11-year veteran of the Milwaukee County district attorney's office. She argued for the judge to sentence Dahmer to prison for at least five to six years. "In my judgment, it is absolutely crystal clear that the prognosis for treatment of Mr. Dahmer within the community is extremely bleak . . . and is just not plain going to work," said Shelton at the sentencing hearing.[4] Three psychologists also spoke at the sentencing hearing. They recommended hospitalization and intensive treatment for Dahmer.

Shelton argued that Dahmer had chosen the 13-year-old boy because Dahmer knew his age would make him an easy target. In her view, Dahmer knew that he was dealing with a child and not a consenting adult. In addition, Shelton was convinced that Dahmer's history made it likely that he would reoffend. She pointed out that Dahmer was already in therapy for lewd behavior that involved children, which had done little to stop his crimes against Somsack. She stressed that to protect the community, Dahmer's treatment should occur in prison.

Dahmer's attorney, Gerald Boyle, asked the judge to be lenient in his sentencing. He praised Dahmer's work ethic and pointed out that Dahmer had not had another

GERALD BOYLE

When Lionel Dahmer needed a lawyer for his son in 1988, he hired Gerald Boyle. At the time, Boyle was one of the best-known lawyers in Wisconsin. He had experience in a variety of cases, including ones involving murder, drugs, child abuse, and police brutality. Boyle was known as a skilled trial lawyer. He was excellent at cross-examining witnesses and delivering a knockout closing argument.

Gerald Boyle, *left*, would go on to represent Dahmer in later trials. Boyle was considered one of Milwaukee's top criminal defense attorneys.

incident since his arrest in September 1988. He asked for compassion, describing Dahmer as a sick man who could be rehabilitated with the right treatment. Boyle stressed that the treatment Dahmer needed was better delivered through the probation department, not a prison.

Lionel Dahmer also spoke on his son's behalf. He told the judge that he had always supported his son and that he promised to continue to help him going forward. Then Dahmer himself spoke to the judge. He admitted that he was an alcoholic and expressed remorse for his actions in the past. He asked the judge for leniency in sentencing and to allow him to continue working.

A Lenient Sentence

Judge Gardner was swayed by Boyle's arguments for lenient sentencing and by Dahmer's apparent remorse. He believed Dahmer would have a better chance of rehabilitation outside prison. Instead of the five to six years in prison that Shelton had asked for, Gardner sentenced Dahmer to one year in the Milwaukee County House of Correction under work release. This sentence would allow Dahmer to keep his job. Instead of a traditional prison, Dahmer would spend his time at a correctional center, which was more like a dorm. He would also serve five years of probation and be ordered to get psychological counseling and alcohol treatment.

In December 1989, Dahmer wrote to Judge Gardner to request early release from his work-release sentence. "I have had a chance to look at my life from an angle that was never presented to me before. What I did was deplorable. The world has enough misery in it without my adding more to it. Sir, I

MILWAUKEE COUNTY HOUSE OF CORRECTION

The Milwaukee County House of Correction, where Dahmer spent less than a year, is a medium security county jail in Franklin, Wisconsin. The jail holds male offenders who have been convicted of offenses under Wisconsin state and federal laws. In 2023, the jail could hold a maximum of 960 inmates.[5]

can assure you that it will never happen again," Dahmer wrote.[6]

Lionel Dahmer was concerned about his son being released early. He feared Dahmer would fail again without adequate treatment for his alcoholism. Lionel wrote to the judge and expressed these concerns. However, the judge granted Dahmer's early release on March 2, 1990. Once again, Dahmer stayed with his grandmother. But she insisted it was only temporary until Dahmer could find another place to live.

WORK-RELEASE PROGRAMS

Work-release programs involve prisoners who the courts determine can be trusted or monitored. They allow a prisoner to leave prison in order to work. The prisoner returns to the prison when his or her job shift is done. Sometimes a prisoner will leave in the morning to go to work and return at night. Other times, a prisoner will be allowed to stay outside the prison during the workweek, Monday through Friday, and return to the prison for a two-day weekend.

In 1989, while at the correctional center, Dahmer was given a 12-hour pass to spend Thanksgiving Day with his family. But he returned to the center reeking of alcohol and failed a sobriety test.

CHAPTER SIX

HOUSE OF HORRORS

Released from jail two months early, Dahmer found a new place to live. It was an apartment in the Oxford Apartments at 924 North 25th Street in Milwaukee. In his apartment, Dahmer had the privacy to continue luring and murdering unsuspecting men. His new apartment was in an area of Milwaukee that kept police busy at all hours of the day and night. It was easy for Dahmer to blend in with his neighbors and operate unnoticed.

A Pattern of Murder

Dahmer quickly fell into a familiar pattern at his apartment. He usually lured a victim to his apartment by offering to pay the man to pose for pictures. Sometimes Dahmer invited the man to watch pornographic videos. After persuading the man to come to his apartment, Dahmer usually offered him a

Dahmer's apartment door had only two locks. He had also installed locks on the bedroom and bathroom doors, along with security cameras inside the apartment.

PREMISES PROTECTED
BY ELECTRONIC
SECURITY
SYSTEM
213
ATTACH TO INSIDE OF WINDSHIELD WITH TAPE - THIS SIDE FACING OUT
Milwaukee Police Department
EVIDENCE
DO NOT HANDLE
Date of Inventory: 7-23-91
Inventory number:
Officers assigned:
District or Bureau: CIB
ATTACH TO INSIDE OF WINDSHIELD WITH TAPE - THIS SIDE FACING OUT

mixed drink, which had been laced with crushed sleeping pills. Dahmer experimented with different sedatives to drug his victims, even using ether, a colorless liquid that was used in hospitals as one of the first anesthetic drugs. The sedatives caused the victim to fall asleep and become unresponsive. Then Dahmer would strangle the man to death, using either his bare hands or a leather strap he bought specifically for carrying out his murders.

Although Dahmer mainly followed a pattern when killing his victims, he soon began experimenting with different ways to get rid of the bodies. He still dismembered his victims, cutting them into pieces. But now he tested different chemicals that could be used to dissolve the body parts. Dahmer decided to use hydrochloric acid. After the victim's body parts had been soaked in hydrochloric acid for a few days, they became soft and sludge-like. Dahmer could then easily flush the pieces down the toilet.

ESCAPE

A few lucky people went to Dahmer's apartment and survived. In one case, a 15-year-old Hispanic boy went to the apartment but refused the drink Dahmer offered him. When Dahmer tried to strangle the boy, he was able to convince Dahmer that he would not call the police. Dahmer let him go. The boy and his mother reported the incident to their social worker, who promised to notify the police. The police visited the family once but never returned. Neither did the social worker. Once again, Dahmer had slipped away without getting caught.

Dahmer also began to keep body parts of his victims. Sometimes he cut off the man's genitals and preserved them in formaldehyde. Sometimes Dahmer used his Polaroid camera, which instantly printed photos, to take pictures of his victims. Once, he waited for his victim's body to become stiff with rigor mortis so that he could photograph it standing up. Dahmer made a picture album to save his photographs.

Dahmer kept some of his victims' heads, as he had done with Anthony Sears. He boiled the heads with a heavy-duty detergent to clean them and remove the flesh from the bone,

Dahmer said he planned to build an altar out of the bones and skulls of his victims. He drew a sketch of his design.

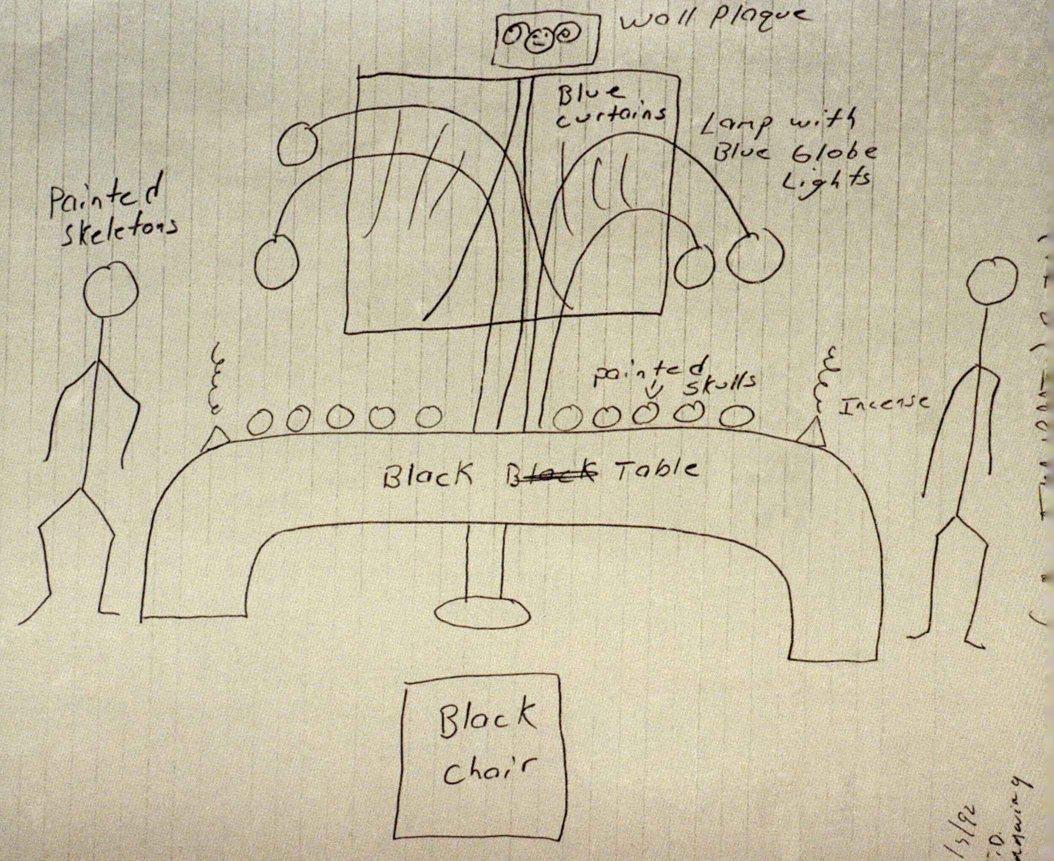

which took a couple of hours. As he had done with Sears's skull, Dahmer covered each clean skull with gray spray paint to make it look fake in case anyone saw his gruesome collection.

Dahmer also attempted to cover up his involvement with the missing men. He cut up their identification cards and jewelry and then threw the pieces away in the trash. But Dahmer was not completely thorough, and the police would later find the IDs of two victims in his apartment.

Probation Officer Meetings

While he lived at the Oxford Apartments, Dahmer met regularly with his probation officer, Donna Chester. This was required under his sexual assault case sentencing. Typically, Chester would be required to make home visits for her clients. However, she requested not to meet Dahmer in his neighborhood because she felt unsafe. As a result, Chester never saw where Dahmer was living.

On May 15, 1990, Chester met with Dahmer the day after he moved into the apartment. They talked about his job, and Dahmer expressed an interest in real estate and potentially taking classes at the local technical college. Over the next year, Dahmer would miss several appointments with Chester. But he always had a believable excuse, saying he overslept or was sick.

When they did meet, Chester and Dahmer talked about his sexual feelings for men, as well as his alcohol problems.

Dahmer told Chester he was not sleeping enough and felt guilty for being gay. Chester suggested he talk to a gay rights organization to help him work through his feelings. But Dahmer assured Chester that he was working too much at the chocolate factory to have unhealthy desires for minors.

Sometimes Chester noted that Dahmer appeared depressed or looked disheveled. Still, she refused to conduct a home visit. And nothing Dahmer said alerted Chester to the horrors that were unfolding at his apartment.

OXFORD APARTMENTS

The Oxford Apartments held 49 units, including apartment 213, where Jeffrey Dahmer's grisly crimes were discovered. The building was demolished in 1992, about 15 months after the discovery of human remains in Dahmer's apartment.[1] In the years since then, efforts to use the space have failed. In 2022, it was a vacant lot surrounded by a fence.

Settling into a Routine

In May 1990, Dahmer killed his sixth victim, a young Black man named Ricky Lee Beeks. The two met at Club 219, where Dahmer lured Beeks back to his apartment with the promise of drinks and money for photographs. Dahmer drugged and strangled Beeks, and then he had sex with the corpse. Dahmer said that by the spring of 1990, he had become faster and more efficient at cutting up bodies. Dahmer kept Beeks's skull, cleaning and painting it.

In June 1990, Dahmer met Eddie Smith, a 28-year-old Black man, at the Phoenix Bar. Dahmer offered to pay Smith to pose for pictures. The two men returned to Dahmer's apartment, where Dahmer served Smith a drugged drink. When Smith passed out, Dahmer strangled him. He dismembered Smith's body, taking pictures during the process. Dahmer loaded the body parts into trash bags and put them in the garbage bins at the back of the apartment building. Smith's remains were never found, but Dahmer later identified him from a picture.

In September 1990, Dahmer met Ernest Miller, a 24-year-old Black man, near an adult bookstore in Milwaukee. Miller accepted Dahmer's invitation to go back to his apartment for money. When Miller passed out from a drugged drink, Dahmer killed him with a hunting knife. He dragged Miller's body to the bathtub, where he dismembered him. Dahmer removed Miller's flesh and threw it out in the trash. He cleaned and painted Miller's skull, adding it to his growing collection. This time, Dahmer varied slightly from his usual routine. He bleached Miller's bones and hung his skeleton in the shower. Dahmer took pictures of the hanging skeleton and kept it.

Now Dahmer had established a routine. Luring the unsuspecting men back to his apartment had become easier.

He refined his methods and gathered all the necessary tools and supplies. By preserving body parts and cleaning skulls, Dahmer felt like he could keep his victims with him forever. They would never leave him.

Cannibalism

At some point in 1990, Dahmer began to eat parts of his victims. In an interview with detectives in 1991, Dahmer explained why he made this choice after one of his killings. "I began to feel that I needed more of a rush. I thought to myself, I want more. I wanted to keep this one, but I wanted him in me. I wanted him to become part of me. That's when the idea of eating part of his body occurred to me. So, I severed his biceps, which were beautiful. I also took his thigh and his heart," Dahmer said.[2]

In September 1990, Dahmer killed his ninth victim, David Thomas. This time, he did not keep any of Thomas's body parts. However, he kept photographs that were later used to identify Thomas as a victim.

Lionel Dahmer speculated that the multiple medications Joyce Dahmer took during her pregnancy with Jeffrey may have contributed to his violent behavior.

From September 1990 to February 1991, Dahmer's gruesome activities slowed. He went to alcohol and mental health treatment programs but made little progress. He worried about seeing his family for Thanksgiving and Christmas because he was ashamed of his behavior. Chester encouraged Dahmer to send a Christmas card to his mother, since he had not spoken to her in five years.

What Is That Smell?

In February 1991, Dahmer killed again. This time his victim was Curtis Straughter, an 18-year-old Black man from Milwaukee. Dahmer met Straughter at a bus stop near his apartment. By May 1991, Dahmer would kill two more victims, Errol Lindsey and Tony Hughes.

Meanwhile, Dahmer's neighbors began noticing the foul odors in the building. The neighbors had many theories about the source of the smell. Some residents thought it came through the heating ducts, while others believed it seeped through the walls. Sometimes the smell would fade away, only to return stronger than ever. Residents wondered if

THE MURDER UPSTAIRS

On May 3, 1991, 28-year-old Dean Vaughn was found dead in his apartment in the Oxford Apartments building. The young Black man was strangled, and his murder remained unsolved in 2022. Some people believe Vaughn may have been another Dahmer victim, since the two men lived in the same apartment building, and since Vaughn died just two months before Dahmer was arrested. However, Dahmer always insisted he was not involved in Vaughn's death.

it was rotten food, smelly trash, or even dead mice in the walls. But they all agreed that whatever the smell was, it was coming from Dahmer's apartment, number 213. Nanetta Lowery moved into the apartment directly above Dahmer's, number 313. She moved out less than a month later to escape the foul smell.

A neighbor who lived down the hall, Vernon Bass, woke up to a horrible smell one night around 2:30 a.m. He covered the bottom of his door with a towel to block the smell and went back to sleep. The next day, his wife, Pamela, investigated the smell's source and determined it was coming from Dahmer's apartment. She waited for Dahmer to come home from work and then asked him about it. Dahmer apologized and told Pamela that his freezer had stopped working and some meat had gone bad. He promised to take care of it.

Dahmer later admitted to detectives in 1991 that the smell was always tricky to manage. "I tried to keep the bodies with me for as long as I could after I killed them, but after a day or so, they started to rot, depending on the temperature of my room. Summers were really the worst because I didn't have air conditioning," he said.[3]

Every time he was confronted about the smell, Dahmer offered an excuse. Sometimes, he said his fish had died or that he had a sewage problem. For more than a year, Dahmer promised to take care of the smell. His neighbors believed him.

CHAPTER SEVEN

KILLING SPREE ENDS

On May 26, 1991, Dahmer met a 14-year-old boy, Konerak Sinthasomphone, at a mall in Milwaukee. The boy was the brother of the Laotian teen whom Dahmer had been arrested for assaulting in 1988. Dahmer offered Konerak money to pose for pictures at his apartment. The boy agreed, and the two returned to the apartment. The teen posed in black bikini underwear for photos, watched videos, and engaged in sexual activity with Dahmer. As usual, Dahmer slipped the teen sedatives in a drink, and the boy passed out.

Dahmer needed more beer, so he left the sleeping teen to go to the store. But while Dahmer was gone, Konerak regained consciousness and fled the apartment. Dahmer's neighbor, Glenda Cleveland, and her daughter, Sandra Smith, saw the naked teen and called 911. "I'm on 25th and State, and there

Philip Arreola was the chief of the Milwaukee police in 1991. He fired the officers who let Dahmer take victim Konerak Sinthasomphone back to his apartment.

WISN
4
4
POLICE

BROTHERS

In interviews with his defense team, Dahmer insisted that he did not know the young boy he was arrested for sexually assaulting in 1988 was the brother of victim Konerak Sinthasomphone. Their family, which included eight children, had immigrated to Milwaukee from Laos in 1979. They immigrated because communists in their home country threatened to take the family's rice farm. The family chose Milwaukee because they knew relatives and friends living in the city, which had a thriving Laotian community.

is this young man. He is buck-naked. He has been beaten up. He is very bruised up. He can't stand. . . . He has no clothes on. He is really hurt. . . . He needs some help," Smith told the 911 operator.[1]

Paramedics arrived shortly after 2:00 a.m. and wrapped the teen in a blanket. Meanwhile, Dahmer returned from his beer run and stood near the boy. Three police officers—Joe Gabrish, John Balcerzak, and Rick Porubcan—arrived at the scene. They spoke to Dahmer, who explained that the boy was his guest and had had too much to drink. Dahmer also told officers that the young man was named John Hmung and was 19 years old. Konerak, still feeling the effects of being drugged, could not give the police a coherent statement.

A Master Manipulator

The officers believed Dahmer when he said the incident was a simple domestic situation that did not require any

Some of Dahmer's neighbors, such as Cleveland, were suspicious of him. But most of his neighbors were shocked to learn that Dahmer was a killer.

police involvement. They escorted Dahmer and Konerak back to Dahmer's apartment. They never ran a check on Dahmer's name. If they had done so, it would have revealed his prior police record.

Inside Dahmer's apartment, the police saw Konerak's clothing neatly folded on the couch. The apartment appeared to be tidy. Dahmer showed the officers the Polaroid photos of Konerak to prove his story. Meanwhile, Konerak sat on the couch as the police spoke with Dahmer. According to the officers, he never appeared to want to leave.

One of the officers noticed an unpleasant smell in Dahmer's apartment. It smelled to him like someone had not flushed the toilet. Behind the bedroom door, the three-day-old body

OFFICERS BALCERZAK AND GABRISH

After Dahmer's arrest, it became known that police had returned teen Konerak Sinthasomphone to Dahmer, essentially ensuring the boy's fate. The officers who responded to the initial call, John Balcerzak and Joseph Gabrish, were fired by Police Chief Philip Arreola in September 1991. The officers appealed the firing, and a judge ruled in their favor and ordered them reinstated. The judge acknowledged the officers' mistakes but said it was unfair to judge them based on hindsight.

of Tony Hughes lay decomposing on the bed, but the officers did not enter the room to investigate the source of the smell. Deciding that no crime had occurred, the police left Konerak with Dahmer in apartment 213.

When the police were gone, Dahmer strangled the teen. He took photos of the boy's body, dismembered it, and kept his skull. Later, many people wondered how the police could have let Dahmer slip through their fingers.

Calls Ignored

Later that night, Balcerzak and Gabrish returned to the police station. While they were there, Glenda Cleveland called to find out what had happened to the boy she had seen on 25th Street. When the officers told her the boy was an adult, Cleveland insisted he was a child. But the police brushed off her concerns.

Cleveland read a newspaper article about Konerak's disappearance two days after the incident. Convinced it was the boy she had seen with Dahmer, she called the police again. She asked them to come to the apartment building and take statements from her and her daughter. "They told me they were investigating a murder and didn't have anyone to send. They said they would send somebody when they had a chance," said Cleveland.[2] But the police never came.

More Victims

Once again, Dahmer had escaped detection. According to Donna Chester's June 1991 notes, Dahmer was attending an alcohol and drug treatment program. He also told her he was not drinking and had not engaged in sexual activity.

On June 30, Dahmer traveled to Chicago for a Gay Pride parade. There he met Matt Turner and lured him back to Milwaukee. Turner became Dahmer's fourteenth victim. After killing Turner, Dahmer put his head in the freezer and his body in the large blue barrel in his apartment. A week later, Dahmer lured another victim from Chicago, Jeremiah Weinberger, a 23-year-old from Puerto Rico. Across Chicago's gay community, worry began to spread that men were disappearing.

Losing Control

Meanwhile, Dahmer was losing control. He found his next victim on the street near his apartment. On July 15, Dahmer met Oliver Lacy, a 23-year-old Black man. He invited Lacy to his apartment, where he drugged and strangled him. Dahmer engaged in sexual activity with the body and then dismembered it. He put Lacy's head in the refrigerator and placed his heart in the freezer, as he planned to eat it later.

After being warned numerous times about his lateness and absences, Dahmer was fired from his job at the chocolate factory in July 1991. He spent the next few days drinking. He visited Chester and appeared upset over being potentially evicted from his apartment. She reassured him and gave him information about emergency housing. Dahmer murdered his next victim the following day.

On July 19, Dahmer spotted Joseph Bradehoft, a 25-year-old white man from Milwaukee, at a bus stop near Marquette University. Dahmer lured Bradehoft to his apartment with an offer to pay for photos and watch videos. Dahmer drugged and strangled Bradehoft, dismembering the body. He put Bradehoft's head in his freezer and placed his body in the blue barrel. Inside the barrel, the bodies of

TRACY EDWARDS

Tracy Edwards was lucky to escape Dahmer. He was called a hero for leading police to the killer's den. Decades later, in 2011, he was sent to prison for a year and a half for his role in the death of a man experiencing homelessness. In the early 2020s, Edwards's whereabouts were unknown, and he was assumed to be homeless. Many believe that Edwards has never recovered from his night of horror in Dahmer's apartment.

Lacy, Weinberger, and Turner were already decomposing. In less than three weeks, Dahmer had killed four men.

One More Attempt

On July 22, 1991, Dahmer tried to murder another young man. But this time, he was not successful. That night in July, Dahmer met 32-year-old Tracy Edwards. Dahmer invited him to his apartment. Once they arrived, things went awry.

According to Edwards, the two men were watching a movie when Dahmer put a set of handcuffs on Edwards. Dahmer kept Edwards trapped while he watched the movie *The Exorcist III*. Edwards told investigators that at one point, Dahmer grabbed a knife and pressed it against Edwards's chest. Dahmer made Edwards lie on the floor so he could listen to his heart, saying he planned to eat it. Dahmer also showed Edwards his skulls, a human hand, and a human head. When he got the chance, Edwards escaped by punching Dahmer in the face. He fled from the apartment and ran down the street until he found nearby police officers.

When Tracy Edwards appeared in interviews and news reports about the Dahmer case, Mississippi police recognized him. They called Milwaukee police to arrest him on an outstanding warrant for not showing up for court.

CHAPTER EIGHT

INVESTIGATION AND TRIAL

After the gruesome discoveries in Dahmer's apartment, investigators faced many unanswered questions. Who were the victims found in the apartment? What had happened to them? And why did Dahmer commit these murders? Now the work would begin as numerous investigators and experts attempted to identify the human remains and build a case against Dahmer.

Identifying the Victims

Once police discovered the crime scene at apartment 213, they called the Milwaukee County medical examiner's office. The medical examiner's office personnel worked closely with the Milwaukee Police Department to gather evidence. They photographed and documented the scene. They collected

In the freezer section of Dahmer's fridge, investigators found a human heart and muscles neatly packaged in bags. In a portable freezer, they found bones and pieces of human tissue.

CHEVROLET
2561

EXPERIMENTS WITH VICTIMS

When Jentzen's team removed the paint from the recovered skulls, they found holes drilled into the bone. Some skulls had two holes, while others had three or four holes. The frozen skull had a single hole in the bone, surrounded by faint blood staining. Inside the skull, examiners found evidence that the head injury was sustained while the victim was still alive. When detectives asked Dahmer about the holes in the skulls, he admitted that he had tried to create "zombies" out of his victims. He experimented by drilling into the victims' skulls and injecting acids and other materials into their heads.

evidence, including tape, a hammer, a handsaw, and an electric drill. They also collected photographs of victims before, during, and after dismemberment.

Detectives collected seven skulls, four heads, four skeletons, and multiple organs from Dahmer's apartment. They sent the human remains to the Milwaukee County medical examiner's office, which was headed by Jeffrey Jentzen. It was Jentzen's job to identify the remains and determine the cause of death for each victim, if possible. To do this, Jentzen assembled a team of experts, including three pathologists, a forensic dentist, and a forensic anthropologist. Although Dahmer was cooperating with police, he could not give them the names of many of his victims.

Jentzen's team examined the body parts recovered from the apartment. They took X-rays and prepared for dental exams of the skulls. They also tested the soft-tissue remains

EXAMINING HUMAN REMAINS

Specially trained experts such as forensic anthropologists gather information, or postmortem data, about human remains. They use this information to identify the remains and determine the cause of death.

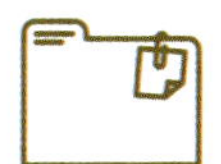

General information such as age range, sex, and height

Medical/dental facts and unique characteristics such as dental work

Evidence of old bone fractures or surgeries

Trauma and post-death damage to the remains

Fingerprint information

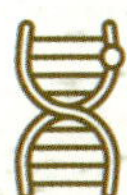

DNA data

Clothes and other personal items found with the remains

Circumstantial information such as where the remains were found, how they got there, and witness statements

and performed toxicology screens to look for traces of drugs or poisons. Forensic specialists examined teeth and bones. Most of the identifications were made from dental records. The team's forensic dentist, Dr. L. Thomas Johnson, had worked in forensic dentistry for decades. He made X-rays of the dental remains and compared them with the dental records of missing people.

Forensic anthropologist Dr. Kenneth Bennett from the University of Wisconsin also worked to identify the remains. First, he tried to determine each victim's ethnic background by looking at distinctive features on the skull. He measured the bones to estimate the victim's height. He also used the bones to determine if the victim was male or female. Bennett's work often confirmed the results of the forensic dentists.

Jentzen's team identified some victims from items Dahmer had kept, such as a county bus pass and a bathhouse identification card. The experts were able to use fingerprints or dental records to identify other victims. They kept handwritten charts that detailed each victim's name, age, body parts, and cause of death. Medical examiners identified 11 victims from body parts found in the apartment.[1]

Interviews with Dahmer

After his arrest, Dahmer talked with detectives for hours. Detective Patrick Kennedy was one of the interviewers. Dahmer described in detail how he lured and murdered multiple men

CRUSHING HOPE

For the families of Dahmer's victims, identifying remains eliminated any hope that their loved ones were still alive. Eleven families were able to get at least part of a body back to bury and grieve. However, for six families, no remains were ever recovered.[4] Dahmer confessed to these killings, but these families never truly knew what had happened to their loved ones.

and what he did with their bodies. Detective Kennedy spent six weeks talking with Dahmer and getting his confession.[2]

Some victims could be identified only through interviews with Dahmer, who admitted to killing six more men. Dahmer's cooperation and confession were an essential part of identifying these men. "He told information on victims that the only way we would have known was for him to tell us. There were no body parts. If Dahmer hadn't assisted, it would have been tougher," said former police captain Kenny Mueller.[3]

In his interviews with police, Dahmer told them about his first victim, Steven Hicks. He drew a map of his family's old property in Bath, Ohio, and showed detectives where he had scattered Hicks's remains. Investigators scoured the area and searched for bone fragments. Martha and Richard Hicks had saved a piece of their son's hair and provided blood samples to help with DNA testing of the recovered bone fragments.

Investigators in Bath sprayed luminol, a chemical that reveals blood traces that the naked eye cannot see, on the floor and walls of the house's crawl space. They found dried blood, a bloody handprint, and hundreds of bone fragments. Testing confirmed the blood and bone were Hicks's.

Meanwhile, dozens of detectives investigated the case. They followed leads and tried to reconstruct each murder. They answered hundreds of phone calls from people who had read about the case or wanted to share information. As speculation increased that Dahmer had traveled the country on a murder spree, he issued a statement through his lawyer. Dahmer said, "I have told the police everything I have done relative to these homicides. I have not committed any such crimes anywhere in the world other than this state, except I have admitted an incident in Ohio. I have not committed any homicide in any foreign country or in any other state. I have been totally cooperative and would have admitted other crimes if I did them. I did not. Hopefully, this will serve to put rumors to rest."[5]

Charged with Murder

On July 25, 1991, Jeffrey Dahmer was charged with four counts of murder and held on $1 million bail. In August 1991, he was charged with an additional 11 murders. In September of that year, authorities in Ohio formally charged Dahmer with a sixteenth murder for the killing of Steven Hicks.[6] He was never charged with the murder of Steven Tuomi because no physical evidence of the crime was found, and the district attorney did not believe Dahmer's statements were enough evidence for the murder.

On September 10, 1991, Dahmer appeared in court with his lawyer, Gerald Boyle. He pleaded not guilty by reason of mental disease or defect to 15 charges of murder.[7] In Wisconsin, a person was not responsible for their crimes if they had a mental illness that made them unable to tell the difference between right and wrong. A person convicted under this plea would be sent to a state mental hospital until a judge or jury determined they were no longer a danger to the community.

A two-part trial was scheduled. The first part would determine if Dahmer had committed the murders. The second would decide whether he was insane at the time of the killings. But the families of the victims disagreed with Dahmer's mental

During his court appearances, Dahmer was reportedly calm and expressionless. He often gave one-word or two-word answers to questions, such as "That's right," "No," and "Occasionally."

defect plea. "I think he knew exactly what he was doing and how he was going to do it. There's nothing wrong with Jeffrey Dahmer," said Inez Thomas, mother of victim David Thomas.[8]

Dahmer changed his plea to guilty but insane on January 13, 1992. As a result, the first part of the trial was no longer needed to determine his guilt. Instead, the trial would focus only on the second part to determine if Dahmer was insane when he murdered the men. The prosecution and defense would make their cases to 12 jurors. Ten jurors needed to agree whether or not Dahmer was insane.

The Trial Begins

The trial began on January 30, 1992. Spectators and reporters gathered around the Milwaukee County Courthouse. "This was the early '90s, so [with the new] 24-hour news cycles, [outlets] were always looking for news to cover, and a serial killer trial was an opportunity that they had to report on. People were waiting in line to get seats or get as close to the courtroom as possible," said Robyn Maharaj, who coauthored *Grilling Dahmer* with Detective Patrick Kennedy, one of the police officers who interrogated Dahmer.[9]

As the details of Dahmer's crimes had been revealed to the public since his arrest, the community was outraged at the poor police response, particularly in the case of 14-year-old Konerak Sinthasomphone. Many people also questioned if police

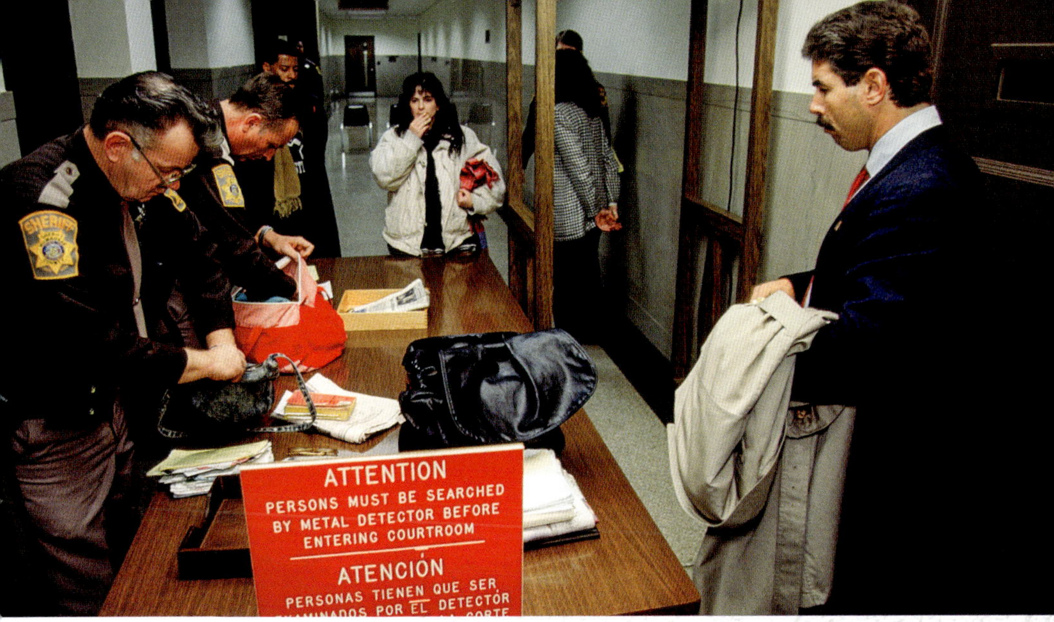

Spectators and reporters attending the trial had to be searched and checked with a metal detector before entering the courtroom. Police also used dogs trained to detect explosives.

bias against people of color and gay men, who were most of Dahmer's victims, had allowed the serial killer to continue his crimes. At the trial, the court was taking no chances. Officials installed an eight-foot (2.4 m) bulletproof glass barrier between spectators and the trial's participants. Before the crowd was allowed into the building, the courtroom was searched for explosives. Family members of the victims, as well as Dahmer's father and stepmother, were given reserved seats.

In his opening statement, defense attorney Gerald Boyle stated that his client was sick, not evil. He admitted Dahmer had sex with dead bodies, committed cannibalism, and attempted to perform lobotomies. "He ate body parts, the purpose of which [was] so that these poor people he killed became alive again in him," said Boyle.[10] But he attributed Dahmer's behavior to necrophilia, a psychological disorder that causes a person to want to have sex with a corpse. Boyle talked about Dahmer's struggle with feeling abandoned. "He wanted to create zombies, people who would be there for him," said Boyle.[11]

Prosecutor E. Michael McCann presented a different interpretation of Dahmer's actions. He said Dahmer was always in control of himself and chose his victims thoughtfully. He killed men to stay in control of them. "His first choice is a totally compliant, living human being. His first choice is not a dead body. . . . He enjoys the bodies for a day or two.

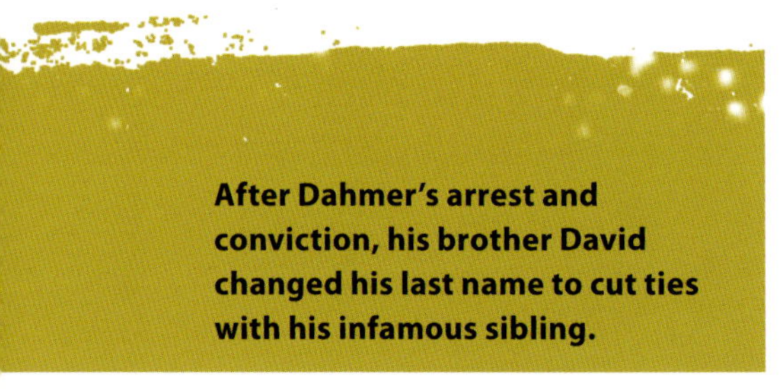

After Dahmer's arrest and conviction, his brother David changed his last name to cut ties with his infamous sibling.

The bulletproof barrier in the courtroom was requested by Judge Laurence C. Gram Jr., who presided over the trial.

Then he tires of it. He doesn't find them sexually attractive. It becomes a disposal problem," said McCann.[12]

Over the next two weeks, the jurors heard gory testimony about Dahmer's actions. Detectives read Dahmer's 160-page confession based on 60 hours of police interviews.[13] They read the details Dahmer had told them about each victim, how he met and lured them to his apartment, and what he did with them before and after their deaths.

Several mental health experts testified about Dahmer's mental state. The defense presented witnesses who said Dahmer's behavior, in their opinions, was evidence of his mental illness. "If this isn't mental illness, from my point of view, I don't know what is," said Dr. Fred S. Berlin, one of the defense witnesses.[14] The prosecution's expert witnesses disagreed, testifying that Dahmer was a killer in control of his actions.

The Verdict

After the prosecution and the defense presented their cases, the judge instructed the jury. First, they needed to determine whether Dahmer had a mental illness. Then, the jury would need to consider if that illness prevented Dahmer from following the law. If the jury found Dahmer sane, he would be sent to prison. If they found him insane, he would be sent to a state mental institution, from which he could eventually be released.

During the trial, some of the victims' family members wore large buttons printed with pictures of their lost loved ones. Many also spoke to reporters, expressing their anger and grief.

On February 15, the jury had its verdict. Ten of the 12 jurors said Dahmer was not mentally ill. Juror Karl Stahle said, "I think [Dahmer] was a real con artist. He could even fool the police and get away with it. I came to the conclusion he was not sick."[15]

Life without Parole

On February 18, Dahmer appeared in court for sentencing. His victims' families were allowed to speak to him and the court. Nine relatives talked about the pain they suffered because of Dahmer. Rita Isbell, the sister of victim Errol Lindsey, called Dahmer "Satan" and shouted obscenities at him.[16]

Dahmer was also granted an opportunity to speak. He apologized to the victims' families. "I know the families of the victims will never be able to forgive me for what I have done. I promise I will pray each day to ask for their forgiveness when the hurt goes away, if ever. . . . If I could give my life right now to bring their loved ones back, I would do it," said Dahmer.[17]

Dahmer also told the judge that he had pled insanity to learn more about his mental state. "I wanted to find out just what it was that caused me to be so bad and evil," he said. "The doctors have told me about my sickness, and now I have some peace."[18]

After listening to all the statements, Judge Laurence C. Gram Jr. announced the sentence. He sentenced Dahmer to 15 consecutive life terms in prison without possibility of parole.[19] It was the maximum sentence the judge could give Dahmer. Later, Dahmer was also found guilty of the murder of Steven Hicks and was given another life sentence. After the sentencing, defense lawyer Boyle said his client did not plan to appeal the ruling. Dahmer would spend the rest of his life in prison.

NO DEATH PENALTY

In 1853, Wisconsin became the first state to abolish the death penalty when the Death Penalty Repeal Act was signed into law. This meant that no matter how horrific Dahmer's crimes were, he could not be sentenced to death. Some state politicians pushed for the reinstatement of the death penalty after the Dahmer case became public. However, after Dahmer's death in prison, the pressure to allow the death penalty lessened.

CHAPTER NINE

LIFE AND DEATH IN PRISON

In February 1992, Dahmer arrived at the Columbia Correctional Institution in Portage, Wisconsin. Because of the publicity surrounding his trial, prison officials initially decided to keep Dahmer away from the prison's general population. This was done for Dahmer's safety. A jail cell eight feet (2.4 m) by ten feet (3 m) became his new home.

Prison Life

Dahmer's life in prison was quiet and routine for the first year, according to prison officials. Each morning, he spent 90 minutes to two hours on work detail, sweeping, mopping, and dusting his unit.[1] He ate with a small group of inmates. The rest of the day, Dahmer smoked cigarettes or watched television in his cell. Sometimes he read or wrote. He was allowed three two-hour

The Columbia Correctional Institution is a men's prison that opened in 1986. It has 500 maximum security cells.

visits each month from people on his visiting list. He was also allowed unlimited visits with his lawyers. Whenever he was out of his cell, a guard escorted him.

After Dahmer's first year in prison, he requested to be transferred into the general population. The move was made when prison officials determined that Dahmer could be safely integrated. But many outside law enforcement officials predicted Dahmer had a target on his back and would not survive the year.

In July 1994, their predictions of violence came true when an inmate attempted to kill Dahmer during a chapel service. The inmate, Osvaldo Durruthy, was in prison for drug and weapons charges. He planned to kill Dahmer even though he had never met the serial killer. He wanted revenge for Dahmer's victims.

Durruthy hoped to carry out his plan during the prison's weekly chapel service. To prepare, he took the blades from his

MAIL AND MONEY

In prison, Dahmer received several letters daily, often from people he had never met. Some letters included money, which he used to buy cassette recordings, magazines, cigarettes, and stationery. One woman sent Dahmer $350 and Bible literature to teach him about Jesus. A nun sent $10 to pay him back for postage on two art books Dahmer mailed her from prison. Dahmer received more than $12,000 from letter writers worldwide, according to prison records.[2]

prison razor and attached them to an old toothbrush handle, making a four-inch (10 cm) shank. He hid the weapon between his shirt and the waistband of his pants. In the chapel, Durruthy maneuvered into a seat directly behind Dahmer and grabbed his shank. "I stood up, with my left arm I put Dahmer in a headlock, and with my right hand, I began to slash his throat with the razor shank. I was slashing him back and forth as fast as I could," he said. "After a few slashes, the shank broke. It wasn't strong enough, it fell out of my hand onto the floor. He was still in a headlock with my left arm, so with my right hand, I started to punch him in the face as many times as I could before prison guards jumped in and pulled me off him."[3]

Jeffrey Dahmer was baptized in prison in May 1994.

Durruthy's plan failed. Dahmer was taken to the prison hospital and treated for minor cuts. For his actions, Durruthy had five years added to his prison sentence. Prison officials determined it was an isolated incident.

A Killer Dies

On November 28, 1994, Jeffrey Dahmer was attacked and killed by another inmate at the Columbia Correctional Institution. That morning, Dahmer was with two other inmates, Christopher Scarver and Jesse Anderson. These two men were also convicted murderers. The three inmates were assigned to clean toilets and showers near the prison's gym. They arrived for work duty around 7:50 a.m., and the guards left the men to clean unshackled and unattended.

Twenty minutes later, the guards returned to find Dahmer lying in a pool of blood on the bathroom floor. He had severe head wounds from being beaten with a metal bar. His head had also been struck against the wall. Dahmer was taken to the prison hospital ward, where he was declared dead an hour later. The guards also found Anderson beaten with the same metal bar, and he died two days later from his injuries. Scarver, who was already serving a life sentence for a 1990 murder, told prison officials that he had attacked the two inmates.

Scarver, *right*, claimed that while the inmates were cleaning, Dahmer poked him in the back and appeared to be laughing at him. Scarver then followed Dahmer into the bathroom and killed him.

DAHMER'S BRAIN

After Dahmer's death, his parents chose to have his body cremated. However, they disagreed about what to do with his brain. Joyce wanted her son's brain to be studied by scientists to determine if anything biological contributed to his actions. Lionel disagreed and wanted to put the entire ordeal behind the family. In December 1995, a judge sided with Lionel and ordered Dahmer's brain to be cremated.

Scarver received two additional life sentences for the murders of Dahmer and Anderson.[4]

More than 20 years after killing Dahmer, Scarver spoke out about his motivations. He said he had grown increasingly disturbed by Dahmer in prison. Scarver claimed that Dahmer would taunt the other prisoners by creating severed limbs out of prison food and drizzling them with ketchup to look like blood. "He would put them in places where people would be," Scarver said. "He crossed the line with some people—prisoners, prison staff. Some people who are in prison are repentant—but he was not one of them."[5]

Reaction to the News

For the families of Dahmer's victims, the news of his death in prison stirred mixed emotions. Some family members felt that Dahmer got what he deserved. Others, like Catherine Lacy, the mother of victim Oliver Lacy, thought that Dahmer's early death allowed him to escape the punishment of suffering in prison.

Lionel Dahmer was devastated to learn that his son had been murdered in prison. Dahmer's mother spoke to the press, saying, "Now is everybody happy? Now that he's bludgeoned to death, is that good enough for everyone?"[6]

Aftermath

The story of Jeffrey Dahmer and his horrific crimes has fascinated people for decades. Numerous books, documentaries, and television shows have explored Dahmer's life and murders. Many of these books and shows are still popular. Serial killers such as Dahmer have attained almost celebrity status. There are Halloween costumes, trading cards, T-shirts, and even college classes that feature notorious killers such as Dahmer.

More than 30 years after Dahmer's arrest, the interest in the serial killer's story continues. In 2022, the streaming service Netflix released *Dahmer—Monster: The Jeffrey Dahmer Story*. The limited series starred actor Evan Peters as Jeffrey Dahmer and presented the story of the infamous serial killer. The series also explored the failures of law enforcement and the legal system, systemic racism, and the homophobia that allowed Dahmer to continue to lure and murder young men for more than a decade.

After its debut, *Dahmer* became a smash hit for Netflix. Viewers spent more than one billion hours viewing the show, making it one of the top three most-watched series on Netflix, along with *Stranger Things* and *Squid Games*. It reached this viewer milestone in only 60 days and spent seven weeks on the Netflix Global Top 10 list.[7]

However, Netflix's *Dahmer* series also sparked controversy. Some people have questioned whether the public needed to revisit the story of a serial killer who targeted Black and brown men. Some family members of Dahmer's victims have also criticized the series, saying it has made them relive the trauma of the murders all over again. They say producers neglected to contact them while making the series.

Rita Isbell is the sister of victim Errol Lindsey. She has been outspoken in her criticism of the Netflix series. At Dahmer's sentencing, Isbell gave an emotional victim impact statement. The Netflix show recreated the statement, casting actor DaShawn Barnes as Isbell. "I was never contacted about

RACISM AND HOMOPHOBIA

For many people, the Dahmer case was an example of systemic racism and homophobia in Milwaukee in the 1980s and early 1990s. Critics of law enforcement say that police failed to pursue Dahmer aggressively because many of his victims were Black and gay. Several families sued the Milwaukee Police Department, saying the officers' racism led to more deaths. They argued that officers' refusal to arrest Dahmer after he was found with Konerak Sinthasomphone, despite the protests of two Black neighbors, was an example of this racism.

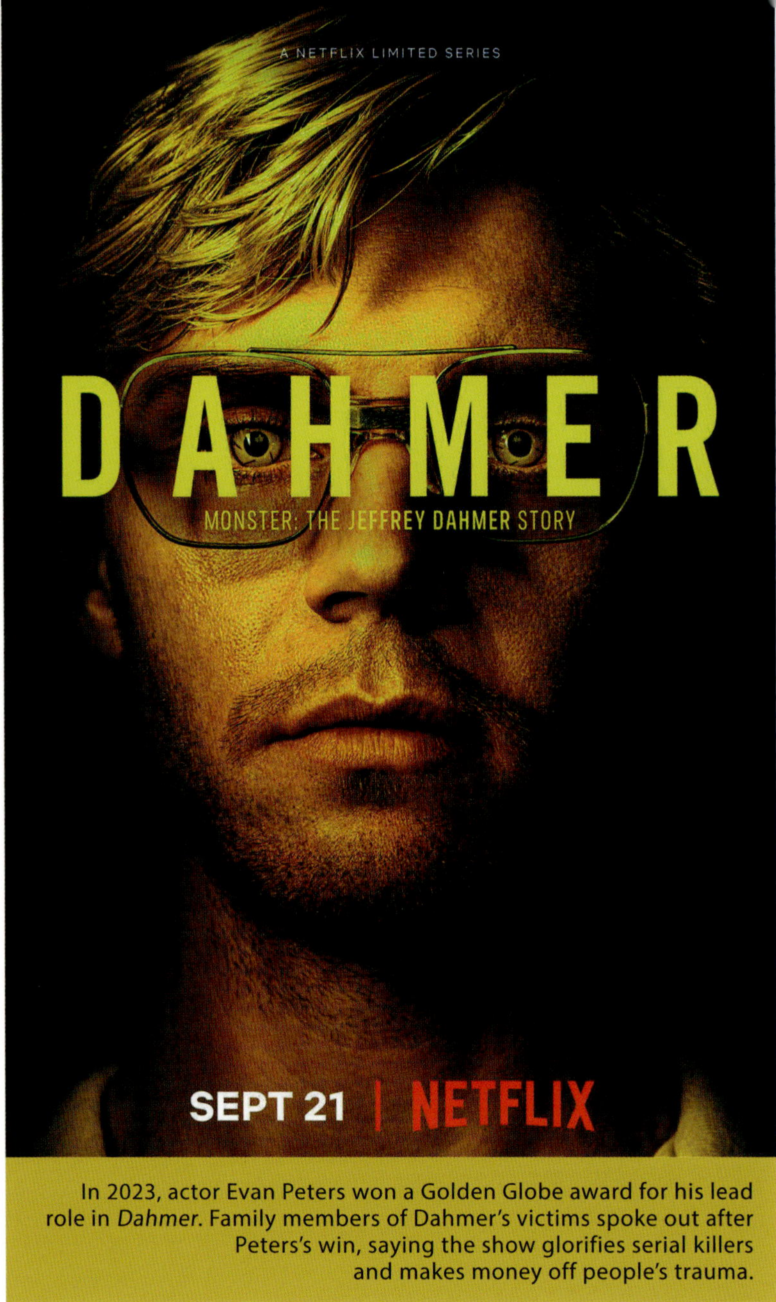

In 2023, actor Evan Peters won a Golden Globe award for his lead role in *Dahmer*. Family members of Dahmer's victims spoke out after Peters's win, saying the show glorifies serial killers and makes money off people's trauma.

the show. I feel like Netflix should've asked if we mind or how we felt about making it. They didn't ask me anything. They just did it," Isbell said. "But I'm not money hungry, and that's what this show is about, Netflix trying to get paid."[8]

A Complicated Man

Jeffrey Dahmer was a complicated man. Many people believed that a serial killer who tortured, murdered, and cannibalized young men was pure evil in human form. Yet those who met Dahmer often described him as mild mannered, soft-spoken, and generally polite. "People always say that I must have seen evil in his eyes as I sat down face to face with him during our interrogations, and I have to honestly tell them that I didn't. I saw a very normal, ordinary guy who—when we talked about things other than his crimes—seemed very much like me, like you, like anybody you would meet," said Detective Patrick Kennedy.[9]

Jeffrey Dahmer was known as the "Milwaukee Cannibal" for his actions.

Unlike many serial killers, Dahmer did not boast about his crimes or try to hide them once caught by police. And Dahmer agreed that he deserved the hatred others felt toward him. In an interview in January 1993, Dahmer told the interviewer, "The person to blame is the person sitting across from you. Not parents, not society, not pornography. Those are just excuses."[10]

TIMELINE

1960

- Jeffrey Dahmer is born in Milwaukee, Wisconsin.

1968

- The Dahmer family moves to Bath, Ohio. Dahmer struggles with feelings of neglect.

1978

- Dahmer graduates high school and kills his first victim, a hitchhiker named Steven Hicks. He buries Hicks's remains on his family's property.

1979

- Dahmer joins the US Army and is assigned to Baumholder, West Germany, in July.

1981

- Dahmer receives an army discharge and returns to the United States.

1982

- Dahmer moves in with his grandmother, Catherine Dahmer, in West Allis, Wisconsin, near Milwaukee.

1986

- Dahmer is arrested for exposing himself to two 12-year-old boys in Milwaukee. He is sentenced to a year of probation and therapy.

1987

- Dahmer kills his second victim, Steven Tuomi, at a hotel.

1988

- Dahmer kills Jamie Doxtator and Richard Guerrero.
- In September, Dahmer is arrested for the sexual assault of a young Laotian boy. Instead of a long prison sentence, he receives a year of work release and probation. He is released after ten months.

1989

- Dahmer kills Anthony Sears and keeps his skull.

1990

- Dahmer kills four more men: Ricky Lee Beeks, Edward Smith, Ernest Miller, and David Thomas.

1991

- In May, police question Dahmer about his involvement with Konerak Sinthasomphone, but they let him go.
- Dahmer's killing spree intensifies with eight victims: Curtis Straughter, Errol Lindsey, Anthony Hughes, Konerak Sinthasomphone, Matt Turner, Jeremiah Weinberger, Oliver Lacy, and Joseph Bradehoft.
- In July, Tracy Edwards escapes Dahmer's apartment and alerts police, who discover body parts in Dahmer's apartment. Dahmer is arrested and eventually charged with 16 murders.

1992

- Dahmer's trial begins, and he pleads guilty but insane. The jury finds Dahmer sane, and he is sentenced to 15 consecutive life sentences in prison.

1994

- In July, Dahmer is attacked in the prison chapel and survives. A few months later in November, he is killed by fellow inmate Christopher Scarver.

2022

- Netflix releases a limited series titled *Dahmer—Monster: The Jeffrey Dahmer Story*. It becomes a smash hit with viewers but also sparks controversy over its handling of the victims' stories.

ESSENTIAL FACTS

SIGNIFICANT EVENTS

- On June 18, 1978, 18-year-old Jeffrey Dahmer kills his first victim, Steven Hicks. The murder is not discovered until Dahmer confesses in 1991.
- More than nine years after his previous murder, Dahmer kills his second victim, Steven Tuomi, on November 20, 1987.
- Police question Dahmer about his involvement with teen Konerak Sinthasomphone on May 27, 1991. Officers return the drugged teen to Dahmer's apartment over the protests of two neighbors.
- Tracy Edwards escapes from Dahmer's apartment on July 22, 1991, and alerts police. Dahmer is arrested, and evidence of his murders is uncovered.
- Dahmer's trial begins on January 30, 1992. He is convicted and sentenced to 15 consecutive life terms on February 18, 1992.
- Dahmer is killed in prison by another inmate on November 28, 1994.

KEY PLAYERS

- Jeffrey Dahmer was a serial killer who drugged, murdered, dismembered, and cannibalized 17 boys and young men between 1978 and 1991.
- Lionel Dahmer was Jeffrey Dahmer's father. He did not see the warning signs his son displayed but repeatedly tried to help Dahmer get his life on the right track.
- Tracy Edwards was a young Black man targeted by Dahmer. Edwards managed to escape from Dahmer's apartment and alert police. Edwards has been praised as a hero for his role in Dahmer's eventual arrest.
- Detective Patrick Kennedy was a homicide detective with the Milwaukee Police Department. He spent six weeks questioning Dahmer and getting his confession, which included details that helped identify the victims.

IMPACT ON SOCIETY

In 1991, the world was stunned when police arrested a serial killer named Jeffrey Dahmer, who had killed 17 boys and young men. As details of Dahmer's crimes were revealed, the public was horrified. Dahmer had drugged, murdered, molested, dismembered, and eaten his victims. Investigators spent weeks identifying the human remains found in Dahmer's apartment and interviewing him about his crimes. Dahmer's cooperation with police was invaluable in identifying many of the murdered men, especially those for whom there were no remains.

The case also sparked controversy, since many people were outraged that Dahmer was able to operate largely unnoticed for 13 years. The Dahmer case highlighted the systemic racism and homophobia that Milwaukee residents faced at the time. Many people believed that the police did not put a priority on finding the missing men because most of Dahmer's victims were Black or gay. In the years since Dahmer's arrest, the public's fascination with the killer and his crimes has continued. There is an ongoing demand for books, articles, and documentaries about Jeffrey Dahmer, as demonstrated by the popular 2022 Netflix series, *Dahmer—Monster: The Jeffrey Dahmer Story.*

QUOTE

"People always say that I must have seen evil in his eyes as I sat down face to face with him during our interrogations, and I have to honestly tell them that I didn't. I saw a very normal, ordinary guy who—when we talked about things other than his crimes—seemed very much like me, like you, like anybody you would meet."

Detective Patrick Kennedy, who interrogated Dahmer after his 1991 arrest

GLOSSARY

anthropology
The study of the origins, behavior, and development of humans.

cannibalism
The act of eating the flesh or body parts of one's own species.

chloroform
A chemical that can cause dizziness, drowsiness, and unconsciousness.

corpse
A dead body.

decompose
To decay and become rotten.

discharge
To release from the military.

dismember
To cut the limbs off a body.

disorderly conduct
A criminal charge for behavior that disturbs the peace, morals, or safety of the general public.

forensic
Characterized by the use of scientific techniques to investigate a crime.

lewd
Crude and offensive in a sexual way.

lobotomy
An operation on the brain aimed at making a patient more compliant.

necrophilia
Sexual attraction to dead bodies.

probation
The release of a prisoner who remains under supervision instead of incarceration.

rehabilitate
To restore to health or normal life by training and therapy.

rigor mortis
The stiffening of the joints and muscles of a body a few hours after death.

sedative
A drug that causes unconsciousness.

specimen
A sample of something, such as tissue or body parts.

torso
The trunk of the human body.

toxicology
A branch of science that involves testing for the presence of poisons.

ADDITIONAL RESOURCES

SELECTED BIBLIOGRAPHY

Davis, Don. *The Jeffrey Dahmer Story: An American Nightmare*. Saint Martin's Press, 1991.

Kennedy, Patrick, and Robyn Maharaj. *Grilling Dahmer: The Interrogation of "The Milwaukee Cannibal."* WildBlue Press, 2021.

Schwartz, Anne E. *Monster: The True Story of the Jeffrey Dahmer Murders*. Union Square & Co., 2021.

FURTHER READINGS

Backderf, John. *My Friend Dahmer: A Graphic Novel, Special Movie Tie-in Edition*. Abrams ComicArts, 2017.

Harris, Duchess, and Valerie Bodden. *Capital Punishment*. Abdo, 2020.

Harris, Duchess, and Kate Conley. *The US Prison System and Prison Life*. Abdo, 2020.

ONLINE RESOURCES

To learn more about Jeffrey Dahmer, please visit **abdobooklinks.com** or scan this QR code. These links are routinely monitored and updated to provide the most current information available.

MORE INFORMATION

For more information on this subject, contact or visit the following organizations:

ALCATRAZ EAST CRIME MUSEUM

2757 Pkwy.
Pigeon Forge, TN 37863
alcatrazeast.com

The Alcatraz East Crime Museum offers information about forensic science and famous cases, such as the murders committed by Jeffrey Dahmer.

AMERICAN ACADEMY OF FORENSIC SCIENCES (AAFS)

410 N. 21st St.
Colorado Springs, CO 80904
aafs.org

The AAFS is a professional society dedicated to promoting forensic science education and improving accuracy and precision in forensic science.

MILWAUKEE POLICE DEPARTMENT

749 W. State St.
Milwaukee, WI 53233
city.milwaukee.gov/police

The Milwaukee Police Department played a significant role in the Jeffrey Dahmer investigation and arrest. Its website has information and news about the department, including crime maps and statistics.

SOURCE NOTES

CHAPTER 1. A GRUESOME DISCOVERY

1. Anne E. Schwartz. *Monster: The True Story of the Jeffrey Dahmer Murders*. Union Square & Co., 2021. 1–2.

2. Schwartz, *Monster*, 3.

3. Schwartz, *Monster*, 4.

4. Schwartz, *Monster*, 4–5.

5. Schwartz, *Monster*, 5.

6. Aly Vander Hayden. "These Are the Chilling Crime Scene Photos From Jeffrey Dahmer's Apartment." *Oxygen*, 9 Nov. 2019, oxygen.com. Accessed 10 July 2023.

7. Isabel Wilkerson. "Parts of Many Bodies Found in a Milwaukee Apartment." *New York Times*, 24 July 1991, nytimes.com. Accessed 8 May 2023.

8. Wilkerson, "Parts of Many Bodies Found in a Milwaukee Apartment."

9. Wilkerson, "Parts of Many Bodies Found in a Milwaukee Apartment."

10. Kelsie Gibson. "'Monster: The Jeffrey Dahmer Story': How the Serial Killer Was Caught." *People*, 22 Sept. 2022, people.com. Accessed 8 May 2023.

11. Molli Mitchell. "What Jeffrey Dahmer Said about Gruesome Killings: 'It Became a Compulsion.'" *Newsweek*, 27 Sept. 2022, newsweek.com. Accessed 8 May 2023.

CHAPTER 2. TROUBLES AS A CHILD

1. "Bone Fragments, Many Human, Are Found at Suspect's Ohio Home." *New York Times*, 31 July 1991, nytimes.com. Accessed 10 July 2023.

2. James Barron and Mary B. W. Tabor. "17 Killed, and a Life Is Searched for Clues." *New York Times*, 4 Aug. 1991, nytimes.com. Accessed 8 May 2023.

3. Daniel Goleman. "Clues to a Dark Nurturing Ground for One Serial Killer." *New York Times*, 7 Aug. 1991, nytimes.com. Accessed 8 May 2023.

4. Anne E. Schwartz. *Monster: The True Story of the Jeffrey Dahmer Murders*. Union Square & Co., 2021. 43.

5. Barron and Tabor, "17 Killed, and a Life Is Searched for Clues."

6. Brian Kates. "Jeffrey Dahmer's Life and Crimes." *New York Daily News*, 29 Nov. 1994, nydailynews.com. Accessed 8 May 2023.

7. Barron and Tabor, "17 Killed, and a Life Is Searched for Clues."

CHAPTER 3. A CONFUSED YOUNG ADULT

1. Jessica Langer. "Retracing Dahmer: Understanding Jeffrey Dahmer's Life at Ohio State." *Lantern*, 26 Oct. 2022, thelantern.com. Accessed 8 May 2023.

2. Debbie Holmes. "OSU Paper Investigates Serial Killer Jeffrey Dahmer's Time at the University." *WOSU 89.7 NPR News*, 10 Nov. 2022, wvxu.org. Accessed 8 May 2023.

3. Langer, "Retracing Dahmer."

4. Sabrina Talbert. "Shari Dahmer Says She's 'Proud' of Her Last Name after Jeffrey Dahmer Killings." *Yahoo News*, 6 Oct. 2022, news.yahoo.com. Accessed 8 May 2023.

5. James Barber. "Why Jeffrey Dahmer Got Kicked Out of the Army." *Military.com*, 27 Sept. 2022, military.com. Accessed 8 May 2023.

6. James Barron and Mary B. W. Tabor. "17 Killed, and a Life Is Searched for Clues." *New York Times*, 4 Aug. 1991, nytimes.com. Accessed 8 May 2023.

7. Beatrice Verhoeven. "Jeffrey Dahmer's Surviving Victims Speak: 'I Thought about Killing Him, I Thought about Killing Myself.'" *TheWrap*, 11 Nov. 2017, thewrap.com. Accessed 8 May 2023.

8. Anne E. Schwartz. *Monster: The True Story of the Jeffrey Dahmer Murders*. Union Square & Co., 2021. 51–52.

9. Schwartz, *Monster*, 52.

10. Matt Bartosik. "Jeffrey Dahmer Could Be Connected to Adam Walsh Murder." *NBC Chicago*, 30 Mar. 2010, nbcchicago.com. Accessed 8 May 2023.

CHAPTER 4. NEW START IN WISCONSIN

1. Anne E. Schwartz. *Monster: The True Story of the Jeffrey Dahmer Murders*. Union Square & Co., 2021. 54.

2. Don Davis. *The Jeffrey Dahmer Story: An American Nightmare*. St. Martin's Press, 1991. 63.

3. Schwartz, *Monster*, 54.

4. Patrick Kennedy and Robyn Maharaj. *Grilling Dahmer: The Interrogation of "The Milwaukee Cannibal."* WildBlue Press, 2021. 54.

5. Kennedy and Maharaj, *Grilling Dahmer*, 57.

6. Kennedy and Maharaj, *Grilling Dahmer*, 61.

CHAPTER 5. ALMOST CAUGHT

1. Anne E. Schwartz. *Monster: The True Story of the Jeffrey Dahmer Murders*. Union Square & Co., 2021. 66–67.

2. Schwartz, *Monster*, 66–67.

3. Patrick Kennedy and Robyn Maharaj. *Grilling Dahmer: The Interrogation of "The Milwaukee Cannibal."* WildBlue Press, 2021. 66.

4. "Police Probe Boy's Return to Accused Killer." *Washington Post*, 27 July 1991, washingtonpost.com. Accessed 8 May 2023.

5. "Milwaukee County, WI Jail and Prison System." *StateCourts*, n.d., statecourts.org. Accessed 8 May 2023.

6. Edward Walsh. "Milwaukee Man Said to Admit 11 Killings." *Washington Post*, 25 July 1991, washingtonpost.com. Accessed 8 May 2023.

CHAPTER 6. HOUSE OF HORRORS

1. J. R. Radcliffe. "The Building Where Jeffrey Dahmer Committed Gruesome Murders Was Torn Down in 1992, and the Lot at 924 N. 25th St. Still Sits Empty Today." *Milwaukee Journal Sentinel*, 22 Oct. 2022, jsonline.com. Accessed 8 May 2023.

2. Patrick Kennedy and Robyn Maharaj. *Grilling Dahmer: The Interrogation of "The Milwaukee Cannibal."* WildBlue Press, 2021. 180.

3. Kennedy and Maharaj, *Grilling Dahmer*, 81.

SOURCE NOTES CONTINUED

CHAPTER 7. KILLING SPREE ENDS

1. Anne E. Schwartz. *Monster: The True Story of the Jeffrey Dahmer Murders*. Union Square & Co., 2021. 96.

2. Schwartz, *Monster*, 101.

CHAPTER 8. INVESTIGATION AND TRIAL

1. Jeffrey M. Jentzen, MD, PhD. "Micro Disasters: The Case of Serial Killer Jeffrey Dahmer." *Academic Forensic Pathology*, vol. 7, no. 3, 1 Sept. 2017, 444–452, ncbi.nlm.nih.gov. Accessed 8 May 2023.

2. Jacquelyn Gray. "Connecting with Jeffrey Dahmer: The Detective Who Grilled the Serial Killer Had Mixed Emotions." *A&E*, 12 Oct. 2022, aetv.com. Accessed 8 May 2023.

3. Colleen Henry. "Years Later: Jeffrey Dahmer Case Still Provides Lessons." *WISN*, 16 Nov. 2011, wisn.com. Accessed 8 May 2023.

4. Anne E. Schwartz. *Monster: The True Story of the Jeffrey Dahmer Murders*. Union Square & Co., 2021. 125.

5. "Dahmer Denies Link to Out-of-State Killings." *UPI Archives*, 28 July 1991, upi.com. Accessed 8 May 2023.

6. Natalie Neysa Alund and Mike Snider. "From the Archives: USA Today's Coverage of the Jeffrey Dahmer Case as It Really Unfolded." *USA Today,* 30 Sept. 2022. usatoday.com. Accessed 8 May 2023.

7. Sarah Kettler. "What Was Jeffrey Dahmer's Murder Trial Like?" *A&E*, 12 Oct. 2022, aetv.com. Accessed 8 May 2023.

8. Schwartz, *Monster*, 157.

9. Kettler, "What Was Jeffrey Dahmer's Murder Trial Like?"

10. Edward Walsh. "Ghoulish Details Dominate as Dahmer Trial Begins." *Washington Post,* 31 Jan. 1992, washingtonpost.com. Accessed 8 May 2023.

11. Walsh, "Dahmer Trial Begins."

12. Walsh, "Dahmer Trial Begins."

13. Robert Imrie. "Detectives Detail Dahmer's Confession at Sanity Trial." *AP News*, 30 Jan. 1992, apnews.com. Accessed 8 May 2023.

14. Kettler, "What Was Jeffrey Dahmer's Murder Trial Like?"

15. Edward Walsh. "Jury Finds Dahmer Was Sane." *Washington Post,* 16 Feb. 1992, washingtonpost.com. Accessed 8 May 2023.

16. "15 Life Terms and No Parole for Dahmer." *New York Times*, 18 Feb. 1992, nytimes.com. Accessed 30 May 2023.

17. "15 Life Terms and No Parole."

18. "15 Life Terms and No Parole."

19. "15 Life Terms and No Parole."

CHAPTER 9. LIFE AND DEATH IN PRISON

1. "Dahmer Slowly Settling into Life behind Bars." *Deseret News*, 23 July 1992, deseret.com. Accessed 8 May 2023.

2. "For a Serial Killer, Money from around the World." *New York Times*, 7 Mar. 1994, nytimes.com. Accessed 8 May 2023.

3. Alan Butterfield. "Exclusive: 'No Regrets. I'd Do It Again.'" *Daily Mail*, 6 Oct. 2022, dailymail.co.uk. Accessed 8 May 2023.

4. Ellie Harrison. "How Did Jeffrey Dahmer Die and Who Is His Killer Christopher Scarver?" *Yahoo News*, 4 Oct. 2022, news.yahoo.com. Accessed 8 May 2023.

5. Harrison, "How Did Jeffrey Dahmer Die?"

6. Harrison, "How Did Jeffrey Dahmer Die?"

7. Anne Cohen. "'Dahmer–Monster: The Jeffrey Dahmer Story' Just Passed 1 Billion Hours Viewed." *Netflix Tudum*, 5 Dec. 2022, netflix.com. Accessed 8 May 2023.

8. Moises Mendez II. "How Dahmer Became Netflix's Most Controversial Show in Years." *Time*, 6 Oct. 2022, time.com. Accessed 8 May 2023.

9. Patrick Kennedy and Robyn Maharaj. *Grilling Dahmer: The Interrogation of "The Milwaukee Cannibal."* WildBlue Press, 2021. 282.

10. Kennedy and Maharaj, *Grilling Dahmer*, 278.

INDEX

ABOUT THE AUTHOR

CARLA MOONEY

Carla Mooney is a graduate of the University of Pennsylvania. Today, she writes for young people and is the author of many books for young adults and children. Mooney enjoys reading about true crime and forensic investigations.